The Best Sex of My Life

a guide to purity

_____

Lindsay Marsh, MD

TRAFFORD

USA · Canada · UK · Ireland

All Scripture quotations, unless otherwise indicated, are taken from the New King James Version®. Copyright © 1982 by Thomas Nelson, Inc. Used by permission. All rights reserved.

Some Scripture references are taken from *The Message* by Eugene H. Peterson, copyright (c) 1993, 1994, 1995, 1996, 2000, 2001, 2002. Used by permission of NavPress Publishing Group. All rights reserved.

Some Scripture references are taken from *The Amplified Bible*. Copyright © 1965, 1987 by Zondervan Corporation. Used by permission.

Some Scripture references are taken from HOLY BIBLE: NEW INTERNATIONAL VERSION®. NIV®. Copyright © 1973, 1978, 1984 by International Bible Society. Used by permission of The Zondervan Corporation.

Some Scripture references are taken from *The Living Bible*, copyright© 1971. Used by permission of Tyndale House Publisher, Inc., Wheaton, Illinois 60189. All rights reserved.

The American Heritage® Dictionary of the English Language, Fourth Edition Copyright © 2000 by Houghton Mifflin Company. Published by Houghton Mifflin Company. All rights reserved.

Note for Librarians: A cataloguing record for this book is available from Library and Archives Canada at www.collectionscanada.ca/amicus/index-e.html
ISBN 1-4120-9157-8

Offices in Canada, USA, Ireland and UK

Book sales for North America and international:
Trafford Publishing, 6E–2333 Government St.,
Victoria, BC V8T 4P4 CANADA
phone 250 383 6864 (toll-free 1 888 232 4444)
fax 250 383 6804; email to orders@trafford.com
Book sales in Europe:
Trafford Publishing (UK) Limited, 9 Park End Street, 2nd Floor
Oxford, UK OX1 1HH UNITED KINGDOM
phone 44 (0)1865 722 113 (local rate 0845 230 9601)
facsimile 44 (0)1865 722 868; info.uk@trafford.com
Order online at:
trafford.com/06-0911

10 9 8 7 6 5 4 3 2 1

Contents

Dedication

This book is dedicated to the Apple of my eye, the Lover of my soul, the Joy of my desire: My Lord and Savior, Jesus Christ. I am nothing without Him!

Acknowledgements

I am extremely grateful for the wonderful support many people have given me during this writing adventure. First and foremost, I honor God for His grace and mercy, and for allowing me to be a partaker of His anointing to change lives in this generation.

Special thanks to Jay and Patricia Hewlin, Esq., Dr. Denise McAllister, Justin Erkins, Whitney Tarver, Pastor Barbara Erkins, Candace Giles, Jennifer Engel, Minister Dietra Wooten, Erica Gandy, Yvonne Orji and Rita Sinha for helpful critique and encouragement. Thanks for taking this journey with me. I appreciate your attention to detail.

Special thanks to my Parents, Dr. and Mrs. Lonnie and Vivian Marsh II. It is my heart's desire to always honor you and make you proud in all that I do. I can not thank you enough for all that you have invested in me! I love you!

Special thanks to my family: Mutha, Trenton, Whitney, Leon, Bryce and Payton. Throughout elementary, middle and high school, undergrad, medical school and residency, you guys have cheered me on. You are the best family a girl could ask for!

Special thanks to my Pastors and spiritual parents, Drs. Mike and Dee-Dee Freeman. I love you for teaching me how to love God, hear God, serve God, honor God and seek God with my whole heart. You are truly the best that the Body of Christ has to offer!

Special thanks to Elder Timothy and Minister Danielle McLean. You will always be my 'home, away from home.' Your family is my family, and I thank you for all of your support and love!

Special thanks to Elder Barry, Minister Laura and Leslie Taylor. Thanks for being my holy hook-up! Destiny is a beautiful thing!

Special thanks to Pastor Jeff and Minister Dietra Wooten, and Ministers Lamont and Tameshiah Shipley. Thanks for your friendship and allowing me to be a part of the youth ministry dream team. This generation will never be the same!

Special thanks to the Word Up! Family, Spirit of Faith Christian Center Family, S.W.A.T. and the *Worth The Wait, LLC* fabulous crew. I am honored to serve you. Thank you for being my #1 fans!

To my husband to be: (whoever you are and wherever you are) I thank you in advance for being a real, transparent man of God, with a heart to serve people. I look forward to being a crown of glory upon your head and enjoying the rest of my life with you!

Foreword

As Senior Pastor of Spirit of Faith Christian Center, a ministry of excellence, I am continually blessed by God's awesome ability to draw people from all regions to this unique body of believers. Lindsay came to Dr. Dee-Dee and I as a freshman from Shaker Heights, Ohio through her roommate Leslie Taylor Williams, when we were still in Anacostia High School, twelve years ago. Pastoring this wonderful young woman of God for these twelve years has been a joy.

If I had to recommend one single book that offers a transparent, face to face, single person's perspective on abstinence, with the power to revolutionize the concept of teenage, college age and young adult sexuality, it would be this book. As Lindsay's Pastor, I have witnessed her transformation from an ambitious teenager into a mature, grounded young woman with a passion to please God and skillfully teach His Word. *The Best Sex of My Life: a Guide to Purity* is her story, her life, her example, and her ministry. She is truly my daughter in the Lord, and I ordained her when she was twenty-one years old, because I sensed the intensity of the call of God and the purpose of God on her life, at such a young age. Lindsay operates in a level of boldness from the Spirit of God that ushers a powerful anointing for change and conviction, in this generation. The same anointing is upon this book, to bring forth radical change and conviction.

I am bible-proud of her contributions to society, as well as the Body of Christ. As her Pastor, I can honestly say that Lindsay adheres to the Word she boldly proclaims on sexual purity. She candidly offers her past stories of sexual compromise, temptation, and sin, to provide wisdom and understanding for the present day challenges surrounding sexual encounters for males and females. She provides the '10 choices to keep you out of trouble', which are a strategic plan from God to perpetuate intelligent decision-making. Thus, equipping the reader with practical advice for remaining focused day-to-day to receive God's perfect plan, one decision at a time. Whether you are 13 or 31, male or female, this book is guaranteed to sharpen you and take you to the next level regarding male/female relationships. Lindsay revolutionizes the concept of virginity, sexual purity and abstinence with skillful flavor and finesse. Therefore, ladies and gentlemen expect to be challenged, corrected and changed. Moreover, expect to be encouraged and empowered to experience the best sex of *your* life, one day, after you have glorified God during this awesome season of your life.

Dr. Michael A. Freeman,
Senior Pastor of Spirit of
Faith Christian Center

Introduction
(Do not skip this!)

Sex. Sex. Sex! Ok. That is all we hear about. I have coined a word for it all: sexploitation. Honestly, the world makes sex look very attractive. It makes sex look sexy. Seductive. From hot, half-naked girls in videos, to the hot, half-dressed men that compose swimsuit calendars, sex sells anything and everything. Being sexy is cool and provocative, however being, not so sexy is seen as abnormal. In our culture it is cool to carry condoms in your wallet or purse, 'just in case'. It is cool to openly display your thong panties from the back of your pants, and it is cool to get drunk and do something stupid that you will definitely need a HIV test for later. However, I believe that it is possible to keep yourself pure until a special day. No, I am not talking about your prom night or the night you decide that you have waited long enough. I am talking about your wedding day! In 2006, it is rare to hear individuals use the words 'abstinence', 'virginity' and 'sexual purity' with understanding and boldness. Why? The word 'virgin' is not a curse word! Allow me to redefine a few words for this book. The word 'virgin', my friends, is a good word. The word 'abstinence', my friends, is an empowering word. Furthermore, the words 'sexual purity' implies a lifestyle that is pleasing to God. Holiness is the new sexual revolution!

I am a 29-year-old doctor, entrepreneur, ordained minister, as well as an attractive young woman whom God has allowed to represent this delicate, yet powerfully provocative message of sexual purity. Do not misunderstand me, either. Yes, I want to get married, walk down the aisle, and all that! Yet, I want the best sex of my life to take place with my husband, not some average dude I temporarily lusted after. Whether you are a teenager, college student or young adult single, God has inspired me to take the time to share some of the knowledge, wisdom and understanding He has given me over the years, so that you can be equipped to experience the best sex of your life, in the days or years to come. This book will address your sex life. Yes, your sex life! In a very non-traditional manner, I will discuss many sensitive issues, from 'tongue kissing' to masturbation. Clearly, this book is not for everyone, but I believe that by divine appointment, you are reading this book. It is my prayer that your life will be tremendously impacted after reading this book. It is my desire that you will pursue sexual purity, as an act of your own will, (not because of your parents, Pastors or mentors), but because you have a real relationship with God, that has translated into a genuine desire to please Him.

Sexual curiosity, sexual challenges, sexual pressure and sexual perversion are rampant among teenagers, college students and adult singles. I believe that part of my purpose in life is to alleviate much of the stress, strain and struggle that stems from sexuality issues, by simply being a transparent example. The challenges, struggles and failures I share in this book are real, yet I share them so that you can gain the experiences and learn the lessons without the headache of actually 'going through' them personally. The creation of this book and *Worth The Wait LLC*, my clothing line which promotes sexual purity with contemporary style and urban class, is my attempt to empower you to be an outstanding single person, with an outstanding testimony. Many of the R&B, hip-hop, entertainment and sports icons of our day have double-standards, professing one thing before their audience and fans, while living a lifestyle that is contrary to their public confession. They profess to 'love Jesus', but their lifestyles are a big disappointment. It is discouraging because many people idolized them and in turn, mimic their poor choices. However, believe it or not, God has called you to be 'the icon'.

Whether you know it or not, someone is watching you at all times, and you have become an example that they follow. It is my goal to inspire you beyond the norm, in preserving your purity, as well as restoring and renewing your purity to its rightful position, which is in Christ. If you are still a virgin, this book is for you. If you have lost your virginity, this book is also for you, too! I am not here to judge anybody. God is greater than our mistakes and misfortunes. God has kept me, only by His grace. God will fully restore and renew *anyone* who seeks complete healing and total deliverance through the blood of Jesus. If you are currently sexually

3

active or promiscuous, and looking for a way of escape, read on! I encourage you to capture the heart of the principles described in this book, and discipline yourself to truly change. If you want 'it' bad enough (change), you will. This is a book about real-life transition, transformation and ultimate triumph for you, regardless of your past!

God is calling you to follow godly examples, in your Pastors and mentors, but he is also developing you as an example for others the follow. I have accepted my calling as a godly example and I want to encourage you to do likewise. It is possible to live holy, be holy and live out the Word of God, while maintaining your 'own flavor' at the same time. It is very possible! When you honor God, He will honor you. I guarantee you, that *"if you seek first the kingdom of God and His righteousness, all these things will be added unto you."* (Math 6:33) God longs to give us the desires of our heart, when we do things His way. (Psalm 37: 4) I am expecting the best sex of my life, because I have made a decision to pursue sexuality, His way.

Honestly, I am not writing this book to ask you to do 'the impossible', but rather I am asking you to take the 'high way'. Isaiah 35:8 states, "A highway shall be there and a road, and it shall be called the highway of Holiness. The unclean shall not pass over it, but it shall be a road for others." Holiness is the sexual revolution to which, God is calling all teenagers, college students and young adult singles. You are reading this book now, because you desire to please God with this radical, yet liberating way of living.

In this book, you will discover:

- my testimony, experiences and challenges with sexual compromise and purity
- how to understand and interact with the opposite sex (from a female perspective)
- holiness: the sexual revolution
- a 10-step practical guide to sexual purity
- the definition of a 'vision', and how to develop your own
- God's original idea for the best sex of your life
- how to be restored and renewed after sexual encounters
- a confession covenant for sexual purity

Living holy, having a pure heart and walking upright before God, are all very important things to God. I pray that this book and the intimate details I share, birth in you a passion for purity, a desire to know Him intimately and a commitment to honor God with your spirit, soul and body. This is a great task, but you can do it, by His grace. I am not perfect, but God does not expect me to be. No one is. However, this transformation into sexual purity begins with a heart that longs to please Him. Let us begin!

My Testimony

Where should I begin? I am the oldest of three. I grew up in Shaker Heights, Ohio, a suburb of Cleveland. My parents were wonderful, providing the best for us. My Dad was a hard-working physician serving the minority community and my Mom was a retired educator, turned homemaker. I grew up in a Black Presbyterian church which offered a church setting, but no form of consistent sound biblical teaching or instruction to bring about change or conviction in my life. However, the foundation of church commitment and involvement was established within me these early years of my life. I remember making Jesus the Lord of my life around the age of 13 because it seemed like the right thing to do. It was a process called 'confirmation', at which time one also became an official member of the Presbyterian Church. In a sense, church was more like a social obligation to us. I was excited to see my friends, especially the boys I liked, and the girls I could gossip with. We went. We sat. We heard. However, no real change ever took place in my life.

When I was 17 years old, I began to change for different reasons. I had a boyfriend that was considered to be my first 'real' boyfriend. No one forgets their first *real* girlfriend or boyfriend. I really thought I loved him. Of course, I also thought that he loved me. I subtly expressed to him, that I was a virgin and planned to keep my virginity until I was married, or at least keep my virginity a little longer. He respected my decision, it seemed. I could not quite articulate why my virginity was important to me. I was a little scared to have sex. I never really talked to my parents about sex. What I learned about sex came from girls in the locker room, my older cousins, television shows, late night programming and a sexual health course that was taught in 5th grade. I did not have any sound biblical doctrine to support my decision, but it just felt right to be a virgin until marriage. My parents raised us, with good moral values, not necessarily Biblical standards. I wanted to protect my virginity because it 'felt' like the right thing to do at the time.

As my relationship with my boyfriend progressed, my standard to keep my virginity began to fade fast as I learned various strategies and techniques on 'keeping my virginity', in my own ability. I mastered the art of having sex, without having sex. Some would call it, satisfaction without penetration, to put it bluntly. The Assistant Pastor at my church, Dewayne Freeman, who does a wonderful teaching entitled, "Integrity Below the Belt", would describe what I was doing as "...getting full off of the appetizers, rather than the main course." Without the Word of God and without the power of the Holy Spirit, I was failing miserably. I had little, to no integrity below my belt. If my very own life depended upon me keeping my virginity, you could say that I was escaping death, daily.

Well, I later discovered that the boyfriend, who was so dear to me, cheated on me. At that particular time in my teenage life, it was quite devastating. Honestly, I truly cried about it in my Mother's arms. I remember it so clearly. I felt betrayed and heart-broken. Yet what the enemy intended for my depression and destruction, God turned around for my good and His glory. Suddenly, out of the desperation of that situation, I began to seek God. I began to truly seek Him and open my heart to Him. Unlike some teens, I never got into drinking and getting high. Surprisingly, I did not become suicidal, depressed or sexually promiscuous as many people do. I simply ran to God. It was a very pivotal time in my life. He literally began to comfort me, restore my peace and heal my broken heart, as it says in the Word (Isaiah 61: 1). God is truly the only One, Who can satisfy the empty void in us, which we attempt to fill with external relationships and things.

I found a book in my house entitled 'Faith to Faith, a daily guide to victory', a daily devotional book by Bible teachers Kenneth and Gloria Copeland. I read this book daily. I read the scripture passages for each day and I became consumed with a desire to know God like never before. As I drew closer to God, He drew closer to me, just as He promised in His Word (James 4:8). It was my senior year in high school, which was already a very stressful time. I was the senior class president, applying to many prestigious schools and taking several exams. Nevertheless, God's presence in my life became more and more apparent as I continued to seek Him. After applying to many schools for undergrad, I fell in love with Washington DC during a visit to George Washington University. I genuinely enjoyed DC, unaware of a divine relationship awaiting my arrival at school. My roommate freshman year, Leslie, befriended me and invited me to her church on the Sunday before the first day of school. This special invitation to church is where I met my wonderful Pastors, Drs. Michael and Dee-Dee Freeman, and became connected to Spirit of Faith Christian Center. God established my relationship with this awesome man and woman of God, and I have been in covenant with them ever since. This ministry was my first encounter with a Bible-believing, Bible-teaching church that taught the 100-fold, uncompromised Word of God in simplicity and understanding. I truly fell in love with Spirit of Faith, my Pastors and the wonderful people I met. I came to realize that this passion to keep my virginity until marriage was inspired by God, and by His grace it was possible. It was possible on a higher level. This level involved an intimate relationship with God, Himself and a desire to please Him.

In time I learned to set up guidelines, boundaries and

a level of accountability in my life. I discovered my value, as Proverbs 31:10 in the Amplified Bible states, "A capable, intelligent, and virtuous woman—Who is he who can find her? She is far more precious than jewels and her value is far above rubies or pearls." As this rare and precious woman of God that God had called me to be, I decided not only to set a standard, but also to *be* a standard that God could use to demonstrate how true singleness can glorify Him. I must admit, it is not always easy. Sometimes, I want to kiss a guy. Sometimes, I just want to be intimate with someone. These feelings are natural, but require the proper context for me to glorify God. Therefore, because I want to glorify God, I am truly excited about being a virgin, and continue to pursue the sexual purity that He expects. I am not perfect! God, by the blood of Jesus, restored those areas where I have fallen short and missed the mark. It took some time, but I love Him for being patient with me.

I continue to wait expectantly for my husband. I want the best, and the best is always worth waiting for. I pray for him consistently, even though I do not know who he is at this particular time in my life. I pray that he is anointed to find me, anointed to pay the price for me and that he is anointed to "dwell with me according to knowledge." (1 Peter 3:7) I have made a very important declaration about myself: I am worth the wait! Yet while waiting, I have decided to make everyday my 'big day'. People always describe the wedding day as the 'big day'. But I have decided that God is big enough and great enough to give me 'big days' all throughout life. God will give you 'big days' right where you are too!

As a single woman I serve my Pastors in various capacities and saturate my life with God's word and His presence. As a result, God has supernaturally caused me to experience wonderful things far beyond what is common for a person my age. I have attended a prestigious university for undergrad and medical school. I was granted the honor of early acceptance into medical school, bypassing the national qualifying exam, the MCAT. I became a doctor at the age of 25. I give God all the glory for opening these doors for me, as I released my faith for His favor. The Bible states that, "...He gives us, richly, all things to enjoy" (1Timothy 6:17). I bought my first Mercedes Benz CLK-320 at age 26 and began building my dream house at age 27. God opened up doors for me, an African-American female to be trained in a white-male predominated specialty, anesthesiology. By God's grace, I am debt-free from all school loans. As a resident physician, I took my Mom on a cruise to the Bahamas for Mother's day, while I took my own private vacation in Las Vegas at the world-famous Bellagio, all in one week. This is incredible for someone my age with my salary and my level of training. These things are not just happening for me because I make 'millions' in my residency program. Absolutely not! Some of you would be shocked to know how little I make as a resident physician. Am I God's favorite? Why would God choose me to do all of these great things? What does *this* have to do with the best sex of my life and sexual purity? Well, God is not a respecter of persons; He is a respecter of faith.

Let me share 'the answer'. It is *not* about 'me'. He longs to do the same for *you*! I have simply made decisions that are in line with the Word of God and the corresponding return is His blessing on my life. I love God with all my heart and I have been serious about my relationship with Him since I was 17 years old. I made some life-changing, principle-based decisions as a late teenager, which I want to share with you in this book. I made the decision to:

1) Guard my heart (Proverbs 4:20-23)

2) Honor my parents, Pastors and mentors (Eph. 6:2-3)

3) Hang with people who have my answer, and get away from people who have my problem (1 Corinthians 15:33, Proverbs12: 26, Proverbs 13:20)

4) Pursue sexual purity (1Thessalonians 4: 3-8)

5) Build my self-esteem around the Word of God (Psalms 139:14-16, 1 Peter 2:9)

6) Go to church, Bible study and sessions that promote my spiritual growth (Hosea 4:6, Romans 12:2)

7) Get a vision for every area of my life: my mate, my education, my profession, my future, my ministry etc… (Proverbs 29:18, Habakkuk. 2: 2-4)

8) Pray consistently (Romans 8: 26)

9) Change my attitude (walk in love) (1Corinthians13: 4-6)

10) Stop *the* sin (1 Corinthians 15:34, 1 John 1:9)

These 10 choices I often refer to as the '10 choices to keep you out of trouble'. These choices helped to guide my thinking and living. We will discuss these 10 principles in detail in chapter 4, because each of them contains a wealth of information to cultivate your journey toward sexual purity, as well.

Mathew 6:33 says, "Seek first the kingdom of God and His righteousness, and all these things will be added unto you." I embraced this scripture and took God at His Word, at the age of 18. I embarked on a journey of learning God's way, God's order and God's instruction. Now, I look back and see that "all these things" have been made available to me, because the Word of God is true. I drive a BMW X5, and live in a gorgeous brand new home with granite counter-tops, hardwood floors, Berber carpet, and a gas-burning fireplace, and I did not have to compromise my sexual integrity to get it! For a new entrepreneur, my clothing line, *Worth The Wait LLC*, which promotes sexual purity with contemporary style and urban class, is projecting to do quite well. I look forward to being able to stand next to *Sean John, Rocawear, Baby Phat*, as well as *BeBe, DKNY* and other leaders in my industry, and give God all the glory! God said that He would do exceedingly and abundantly above all we can ask or think, right? (Eph. 3:20) I just like to believe God for the impossible. I share the following accomplishments, not to make myself appear to be great and marvelous, but rather to let you know that He wants to cause your dreams to come true! As your Heavenly Father, God really does want you to have the best things in life, but your lifestyle must *qualify* for His best. Sexual purity is the lifestyle that qualifies you for God's best.

2

My Personal Experiences

I love men. I always have, but I have learned to love my relationship with God even more. From passing notes in 2nd grade, to wearing matching jeans with a boyfriend in 3rd grade, to lying to my Mother just to sneak over a boyfriend's house: I have always liked guys. As a youngster, I recall playing 'hide and seek', 'house' or other little games that allowed inappropriate exposure for premature experimentation. This behavior was fueled by curiosity. Kids always want to do what they *see* the 'grown-ups' doing. Whether in person or on the television screen, as children growing up, we are like little sponges, absorbing appropriate as well as inappropriate information. I recall the images from television, movies, music videos, and magazines influencing my negative behaviors even as a very young child. In retrospect, everybody was playing the 'kissy-kissy, touchy-touchy game' even as kids. Then when we graduated to middle school and high school, it became 'spin the bottle' or 'truth or dare'. These games, by the way, were especially popular at church retreats and conferences. Scary! Thank God for the blood of Jesus, because if you were like me, you did some crazy, experimental stuff, even as a kid.

Again, I love men. There have been young men who liked me, as well as those who rejected me. I am an African-American woman, so I went through the 'light-skin' boy phase, the 'dark-skin' boy phase, the 'preppy' phase, the 'athlete' phase, the 'rough-neck' phase and the 'multi-ethnic' phase. All of these phases cycled through me, by the age of 19. There is a natural inclination for a girl to like a boy and for a boy to like a girl. Men like women and women like men. My focus is to help you develop the ability to manage these natural emotions, desires and thoughts through the assistance of the Holy Spirit and your relationship with Him. This can be easier said than done it seems, however, God has given me some practical ways in which we can stay on course with respect to 'the opposite sex' that we like so much. We will go over the details later on in another chapter. (Chapter 4: A Guide to Purity)

I am 29 years old, and I am a virgin (technically.) No offense intended, but I am not fat, ugly, or stupid. I write this, because one would only assume that I am still a virgin because I was never granted the golden opportunity to 'get some' when

I was in high school, undergrad or medical school. Trust me. The opportunities have been there, in abundance, and some opportunities I have taken advantage of in the worst way. I would like to share a few stories with you throughout this book, so that you can understand more about my personal journey of sexual purity.

Unfortunately, my first real kiss occurred in my parents' house. I successfully snuck this guy into the house while my parents were out of town and my sitter actually allowed it. (Bad sitter!) The first kiss experience was unforgettable! I had no idea what I was doing. For that reason alone, it was also very embarrassing! His tongue was in my mouth turning flips and tricks and I just sat there, clueless. It was pretty pathetic, but I was only 13 years old and I had no business kissing him in the first place. That was the first and the last time I kissed him! We often think of a kiss as something minor in comparison to sex. However kissing, rubbing, touching, humping and other things that bring about gratification prepare the body mentally and physically for the next step, which is sexual intercourse. God created this process. God created hormones and bodily secretions! This is all a part of God's creative design of the human body and human sexuality.

One kiss *today* may not lead to sex *today*, true. But, it definitely plants seeds for a future harvest of that nature and, "God is not mocked. Whatsoever a man sows, that shall He also reap." (Gal. 6:7) The Holy Spirit began to minister to me about a relationship I needed to sever while away in college. Although I was not technically having sexual intercourse with him, I had mastered the art of 'feeling good' without having sex. In other words, I would call it satisfaction without penetration. I could still walk away from his bedroom with my 'virgin card'. Many Christians have adopted this self-destructive, hypocritical pattern. I was still out of the will of God, despite still being a 'virgin' by technical standards. I had twisted, distorted guidelines. As my Pastor told me, the law of diminishing returns says that "when something ceases to accomplish what you want it to accomplish, you search for more." In other words, the kissing game grew old and boring for me with time, and a new desire to progress onward from kissing to touching, rubbing and intercourse, grew stronger. Without warning you may find yourself proceeding from one level to the next searching for more satisfaction and gratification. It is a very deceptive path into sin. I have been there!

Proverbs 14:16 states, "There is a way that seems right to a man, but its end is the ways of death and destruction." This information may seem totally radical or maybe ridiculous, but in all honesty your understanding of this process and its design to lure you off track has the ability to protect you from straying from God's best plan for your life. Proverbs 6:27-28 states, "Can a man take fire into his bosom and his clothes not be burned? Can one walk on hot coals, and his feet not be seared?" The average teenager or single person always says, "I can handle it." That is exactly what I said. "I can handle a little kissing, or…I can handle a little rubbing, every now and then… no big deal." However, to God, it is a big deal! Truly, your body is the temple of the Holy Spirit if you are a born-again believer of the Lord Jesus Christ. 1Corinthians 6:17-20 states,

"But he who is joined to the Lord is one spirit with Him. Flee sexual immorality. Every sin that a man does is outside of his body, but he who commits sexual immorality sins against his own body. Or do you not know that your body is the temple of the Holy Spirit who is in you, whom you have from God and you are not your own? For you were bought at a price; therefore glorify God in your body and in your spirit, which are God's."

I went from 'kissing to rubbing to humping' to achieve some level of satisfaction in my 'flesh', without realizing that the 'flesh' is never satisfied.

Let me be real. If you are saved and single, sexual intercourse, sexual acts, sexual perversion and 'the like', are dangerous grounds for you. The Father's loving heart toward His children is to prevent STD's, unwanted pregnancies, psychological/emotional damage, ungodly attachments, derailment of divine purpose and unnecessary 'drama' in your life. The enemy would love an open door of opportunity through your sexual experimentation, to steal, kill and destroy (John10: 10) any aspect of your life. He will destroy your dreams, goals for higher education, professional endeavors, and your virginity while infecting you with HIV, all in one blow. Did you know that repeated abortions make a woman more susceptible to miscarriages and failed pregnancies, later in life? Did you know that some STD's can cause sterility and affect your ability to conceive children later in life? The devil would love to silence your testimony for Jesus Christ. Nobody listens to a hypocrite. Nobody listens to a freak. It is amazing to me that this society spends millions of dollars promoting sexual education, STD education, condom distribution, and contraceptives without truly highlighting the fact that you could solve this dilemma with abstinence. Everybody is *not* doing it! Holiness, the sexual revolution, is what I live by. God's way is always best.

I am not telling you something that I am experimenting with. I am sharing something that I live on a daily basis. When I was eighteen years old, I heard a teaching on the 'Priceless Woman.' Proverbs 31:10 in the Amplified Bible states, A capable, intelligent, and virtuous woman—who is he who can find her? She is far more precious than jewels and her value is far above rubies or pearls." I had no understanding of who I was in Christ. I thank God that as I heard His word, a desire to be this virtuous woman was ignited on the inside of me. I made a decision then, that I still live by now.

It has not been a perfect journey for me. I took a wrong turn my senior year of college, in a relationship, which led to several unwise choices, moments of regret and heartache for me (even as a so-called mature Christian). The dangerous part about this relationship was that due to my previous exposure to escalating levels of sexual sin, I had a predisposition to escalate to other levels of sexual sin, at a faster pace than before. For example, if it took me 6 months to advance from 'kissing to playful touching' the first time, this time it took only 1 week. I had been preconditioned for that particular sin. But by God's grace, I got back on track, and continued my walk with Him. It has been seven years that I have truly been walking in sexual purity (no kissing, petting, humping, rubbing, touching…nothing.) Glory to God! This is not a message for perfect people. This is a message for those who desire truth and transformation!

3

Male/Female Interactions: a message for the men (and women)

Ok fellas. This chapter is for you. (Ladies, please read along). As your sister in Christ, I have taken the awesome task of giving you the official 'real deal' as it pertains to your beautiful sisters in Christ. I believe that I have some insightful information to help shape the perspective you should have at this particular season of your life. Until a man and woman are pronounced husband and wife in the covenant of marriage, they are truly brother and sister before the eyes of the God. After accepting Jesus Christ as your Lord you become a child of God, who is your Heavenly Father. Essentially, our behavior toward one another should reflect such a relationship. The Lord has really brought this to light for me in my relationship with my biological brother. We have the same Mother and Father. We are very close in age, and have grown to become very close friends. He is very protective of me in many ways. We hang out together, watch movies, talk on the phone, enjoy one another's company and confide in one another.

One thing I have noticed, however, is that my brother has never tried to touch me inappropriately. He has never tried to kiss me, mouth to mouth, to convey some amount of passion and affection that he has for me. I have never felt uncomfortable around him, and his body language has never projected inappropriate sexual gestures toward me. Some of you are reading this passage and thinking to yourself, "Of course not Lindsay! He is your brother for God's sake, why would he? It would be incest. That is so nasty!" Yes, exactly. It would be nasty, and it would be incest. This is my point. I wonder if our Father God must feel the same way when his children are behaving in a similar manner. I notice some brothers attempting to be clever and casually touchy with their sisters, and some sisters trying to flirt and entice their brothers. This does not lead to activities that please God. Trust me. I have been in both positions. I have had a so-called brother in Christ slowly pressure me over time, to do physical things that I never wanted to do, and I have also played the role of the sister who wore the tight jeans or short skirt on purpose to get a certain guy's attention. 1 Thessalonians 4:3-6 states,

"For this is the will of God, your sanctification: that you should abstain from sexual immorality: that each of you should know how to possess his own vessel in sanctification and in honor, not in the passion of lust, like the Gentiles who do not know God; that no one should defraud his brother in this matter..."

The will of God is our sanctification. The will of God is holiness, the sexual revolution.

When I think of a 'revolution', I think about high school history class which introduced me to historical events like the American Revolution and the French Revolution. These were intense battles, where countries fought for the abrupt overthrow of a government or a sudden change in the system that confined them. God has also called us to engage in a revolution for the abrupt overthrow of the world's view of sexuality. He is calling for a sudden change in the system that you allow to govern your decision-making and interactions with the opposite sex. He is calling you to this sexual revolution, holiness. Holiness leads to the abrupt, sudden overthrow of lust, perversion and ungodly desires. A definition for holiness is, to be dedicated, consecrated, and set-apart to or for sacred use from all unholy or unclean things. Holiness is not your 'do', but your 'who'. It is not in the long skirts, lack of make-up and 'unpierced' ears. It is a lifestyle mandatory for those who want God's best in their lives. You are called to this 'high way' or higher way of living.

Strong's Exhaustive Concordance of the Bible explains the root meaning of this word 'sanctification' to mean, purification, (the state of) purity, holiness. God's ultimate goal for our relationships is purity. He loves a pure heart. Pure motives. Pure intentions. If your primary goal in a relationship is to simply have sex with a female, something is wrong with your thinking. If your primary goal as a female is to give a guy an erection or tease him through your enticement, something is wrong with your thinking. We must learn to respect one another.

As a sister to my brothers in the Lord, I have learned "to possess my vessel (body) in sanctification and honor". I dress tastefully and appropriately. I am trendy with a high-fashion sense, but I never allow the current trends to compromise my integrity before God and my brothers in Christ. I would never want the exposure of my cleavage or upper thigh to cause my brother to stumble, or mislead him in any way. I fully support being a diva, but never at the expense of discounting my witness for the Lord Jesus Christ. My clothing line *Worth The Wait LLC*, boasts of promoting sexual purity with contemporary style and urban class. I am proud to say that. It is common knowledge that men are stimulated by 'what they see' while women are stimulated by 'touch.' Therefore gentleman, maybe you should be a bit more conscious about how and where you touch young ladies. Sometimes, holding hands, massaging backs, and innocent hugging can ignite an unintentional flame that can cause a forest fire! Likewise ladies, the mini-skirts, booty-shorts, and low-rise jeans may give your friend the wrong impression. Is it your motive to draw attention to your body? With this in mind, we should protect one another. As a young man, how would you expect another young man to treat your sister or daughter? Well, do likewise to God's daughters, who are your sisters. That is usually a good standard to keep. Society says, "What goes around comes around", but the Word says it this way, "Do not be deceived: God cannot be mocked. A man reaps what he sows." (Gal. 6:7 NIV) Are you sowing bad seed, with some of your actions and gestures?

I recognize that some women however, are simply crafty. Today, we would use the term 'shady'. Here is a great text about a woman that you should avoid, men. (Ladies, this is a woman that you should never become!)

Proverbs 7: 6-27 states:

For at the window I looked through the lattice, and saw among the simple. I perceived among the youths, a man devoid of understanding, passing among the street near her corner; and he took the path to her house in the twilight of the evening, in the black and dark night. And there a woman met him, with the attires of a harlot, and a crafty heart. She was loud and rebellious. Her feet would not stay at home. At times she was outside, at times in the open square, lurking at every corner. So she caught him and kissed him; with an impudent face she said to him: 'I have peace offerings with me; today I have paid my vows. So I came out to meet you. I have spread my bed with tapestry, colored coverings of Egyptian linen. I have perfumed my bed with myrrh, aloes, and cinnamon. Come, let us take our fill of love until morning; Let us delight ourselves with love. For my husband is not at home; He has gone on a long journey. He has taken a bag of money with him. And will come home on the appointed day.' With her enticing speech she caused him to yield, with her flattering lips she seduced him. Immediately he went after her as an ox goes to the slaughter, or as a fool to the correction of the stocks, till an arrow struck his liver. As a bird hastens to the snare, he did not know it would cost him his life. Now therefore, listen to me, my children; Pay attention to the words of my mouth: Do not let your heart turn aside to her ways. Do not stray into her paths; for she has cast down many wounded, and all who were slain by her were strong men. Her house is the way to hell, descending to the chambers of death. (Proverbs 7: 6-27)

What a powerful message full of wisdom for us to follow. Please learn from this young man's life, to prevent the same episode from occurring in your own life.

The Bible carefully describes a few things that young men should be aware of in such a woman. This woman possessed:

- the attire of a harlot
- a crafty heart
- a loud and rebellious attitude
- enticing speech and flattering lips.

In summary, her clothing, her attitude, her motives, her speech and her game were all a trap. This woman can be dressed in different packages, (from hair color, complexion, height, weight, eye color, shape, ethnicity, style) but the trap is always the same. However, notice that this passage in Proverbs ends with a poor choice because this young man was void of understanding. His lack of understanding caused him to make a series of poor choices that put him into a position of defeat, death and destruction. Unfortunately, the scripture goes on to detail how this particular young man did not know that this encounter "would cost him his life." I wonder if the young man in this passage contracted syphilis, gonorrhea or chlamydia. Possibly, he contracted HIV. If this man was married, certainly his wife and children were jeopardized. If we dig deeper, we may find that this encounter destroyed his relationship with God, which is a much greater tragedy than any disease. Have you ever compromised and sinned sexually, whether it was sexual intercourse, or any of the four-play appetizers that precede the main event, as a Christian? I have. I felt absolutely miserable afterwards. It hurt me, to hurt God. I felt as if my entire relationship with God was completely destroyed. I felt as if those few moments of pleasure would cost me, my life. What misery, anguish and pain. God has better for us!

Let us investigate a little deeper into how this situation happened in Proverbs 7, so that we can avoid any future incidents of a similar nature.

#1) The young man lacked accountability.

"Passing along the street near her corner; and he took the path to her house in the twilight, in the evening, in the black and dark night." Words like 'black, dark, evening and twilight' implicate a lack of God's presence, involvement or sanctioning. Proverbs 3:5-6 says, "Trust in the Lord with all your heart. Lean not unto your own understanding, but in all your ways acknowledge Him, and He will directly your paths." I can not imagine that this young man acknowledged the Lord before going to this woman's house. When I would sneak over my boyfriend's house in times past, I never acknowledged God. Reason #1. I had my own agenda. Lindsay wanted to do what Lindsay wanted to do. Forget about God! Forget about Jesus! Forget about the Holy Spirit! I was trying to fulfill *my own fleshy/freaky agenda*. Reason #2. Religion ruled my life. I did not have a real relationship with God. I had church attendance covered, but I did not know how to let the Holy Spirit lead and guide me into all truth (John 16:13).

Years later in my Christian walk, I learned to sneak my new boyfriend into town without telling my spiritual parents, Elder Tim and Minister Danielle, that he was even coming. Who are we kidding, here? When we do things in secret and without accountability, we are headed in the wrong direction. That is why God gives us Pastors, parents, mentors, leaders, ministers, etc...to help guide us, teach us God's ways, assist in decision-making, and prepare us for moments when we will need to be mature enough to choose the voice of the Holy Spirit over the voice of our flesh (emotions, hormones, feelings). Trust me folks, I am a young adult, (good and grown), but I still ask my parents, Pastors and spiritual parents, what they think about certain guys that I like, or that I am attracted to. Be smart. Be accountable!

Proverbs 15:22 states, "...Without counsel, plans go awry,

but in the multitude of counselors they are established. Proverbs 11:14 states, "Where there is no counsel, the people fall: but in the multitude of counselors *there is safety.*" They may see, hear, perceive and discern something about your 'friend' that you constantly overlook. Usually we are so infatuated and 'in love', that we are blinded by our own emotions. It is for my own good, that I incorporate mentors and ministers into my decision-making process, especially when it comes to male/female relationships. I highly recommend that you do the same. It is challenging at times, but I even listen to them, when they tell me things I would rather not hear. I do not always like *what* they say, but I respect their position and perspective in my life. I would advise you to select a mentor with sound wisdom, advice and maturity. A mentor should be someone who has demonstrated a pattern of good works in his/her lifestyle, and displays a genuine interest in your personal growth and development. For these reasons, Pastors, parents, ministers and the like, usually make excellent mentors. Accountability is a must!

#2) *The young man lacked understanding.*

Dr. Michael Freeman's definition for 'understanding' is "divine comprehension in my heart that gives me the ability to repeat something at will." Proverbs 4:7 states, "…In all your getting, get understanding." Understanding is powerful. This young man may have had a strong, growing relationship with the Lord at one point, but he lacked the ability to maintain it. He lacked the divine comprehension or insight required to withstand this temptation, over and over again. He lacked understanding surrounding the 'sin process.' Sin is presented and packaged in a very enticing, deceptive manner, however, the "wages of sin is death" (Rom 6:23). Sin is designed to be attractive and pleasurable, and then destroy us. Destroy our health, our testimony, our relationships, our self-esteem and our destiny. He lacked understanding about how his present choice to disobey God, was affecting not only him, but also his future children. (Deuteronomy 30:19) He lacked a true understanding of who he was in Christ. You are not a pimp, player, baller or hustler. You are a man of God!

Enticement and seduction were the crafty woman's main devices. The Bible commands us to "Flee from sexual immorality. All other sins a man commits are outside his body, but he who sins sexually sins against his own body." (1 Corinthians 6:18) As soon as he met this woman, he should have started running. She was not meeting him on the corner for a Sunday school lesson; she was meeting him on the corner to 'get into his pants', and probably his wallet, too. Most loose women have a greater motive in mind when seducing a man, whether it is 'gold-digging,' 'wife-status,' entrapment with pregnancy, notoriety, or a sugar daddy incentives. The question is, are you man enough to run from a demonic trap wrapped up in a pretty package? Joseph was. In Genesis 39, Joseph literally ran away from an open invitation 'booty-call' from Potifer's beautiful wife, in broad daylight. The Bible commands us 'to run' because even God Himself recognizes that the pull of sexual persuasion is so strong, that unless you actually run/leave/exit from the situation, you may end up doing something you may regret later. Is it really worth it?

#3) *The young man lacked vision.*

If this young man had prepared a vision for his future wife, he would have never pursued this encounter with the 'Proverbs 7 gold-digger'. The passage describes her as loud, rebellious, crafty, sneaky and seductive. Furthermore, her clothing was scandalous. (Most loose women have very revealing attire!) My Pastor constantly admonishes us, "People will address you by the way you are dressed!" Ladies and gentleman, you will be labeled by your attire. If you dress like a 'super freak' or a 'roughneck', expect for people to respond accordingly. Do not act surprised or offended. Displaying your cleavage and thongs, speaks volumes about who you really are or are not! I imagine that the woman in Proverbs 7 was probably very skillful at using her attire and sexual gestures to tease men. Do you know someone like this? Vision would have put an end to this encounter between the young man and the seductive woman. In a later chapter, I speak about the importance of having a vision. Even if his vision for a future mate consisted of only four qualifications:

- being a Christian,

- loving God,

- having a pure heart (and)

- possessing a purpose-driven mentality;

The woman on the corner would have been disqualified from the onset. A vision will guide you, direct you and keep you from outside distractions and imitations.

4

A Guide to Purity
(the guide of 'how to')

Now as I stated earlier, I love men. Yet, God has given me some practical ways to balance my emotions, desires and thoughts concerning my sexual desires. Sex is God's idea! However, until you are ready to experience this special gift that God has created for you and your mate in the season of marriage, He has set up guidelines and instructions to *protect* you, not to torture you. He loves you! These guidelines are spiritual principles, some more basic than others. My goal is to help you develop the ability to manage your own natural emotions, desires and thoughts by instituting a few guidelines to help keep your 'flesh' in check.

Guidelines are a great thing. Guidelines exist solely for our protection. Guidelines on our public streets assist drivers to stay in their own lanes and help to prevent motor vehicle accidents. Guidelines used in the hospital help prevent the transmission of communicable bacteria and viruses. Guidelines are always there to help us, protect us and create a safe environment. Thus, they help prevent accidents, mistakes and catastrophes. A car accident is a mistake, which turns into a catastrophe, especially if someone is killed. Accidentally contracting HIV or tuberculosis is a catastrophe, especially when someone dies. Guidelines are never used to hinder us or stunt our productivity. They help prevent accidents, mistakes and catastrophes. These next ten principles are my *'how to'* suggestions to prevent accidents, mistakes and catastrophes in your sexual life. I can not write a book about sexual purity and holiness, the sexual revolution, without giving you the 'how to' guidelines. Here are my top ten:

1) Guard your heart

2) Honor your parents/Pastors/mentors

3) Hang with people who have your answer, and get away from people who have your problem

4) Pursue sexual purity

5) Build your self-esteem around the Word of God

6) Decide to come to church, Bible study and sessions that promote spiritual growth

7) Get a vision: mate, school, profession, future, ministry (chapter 5)

8) Pray consistently

9) Change your attitude (walk in love)

10) Stop *the* sin

As I said earlier, I call this list '10 choices to keep you out of trouble', but this is really a list of ten quality decisions that promote purity-driven, purpose-driven and principle-driven living . Holiness will come as a result of your decision to glorify God on a day-to-day basis. It is a process. Do not become frustrated with the process. As my Pastor says, "...trust the process." You are on the road to the best sex of your life, because this journey begins with a pursuit of purity and obedience, one choice at a time.

GUARD YOUR HEART

Guarding your heart is my fancy way of stating the importance of being mindful of the things you allow yourself to hear, as well as the things you allow yourself to see. Guarding your heart encompasses a principle which is found in Proverbs 4:21-23. It states,

> "My son, give attention to My words. Incline your ear to my saying. Do not let them depart from your eyes. Keep them in the midst of your heart, for they are life to those who find them and health to all their flesh. Keep your heart with all diligence, for out of it spring the issues of life."

This scripture begins with a key phase. "My son, give attention to My words." When you give someone or something your attention, it requires your listening skills and your visual/mental ability to focus on what is before you. I remember as a child, my Mom would say, "Lindsay, pay attention to me!" Those were code words for, "Be quiet, close your mouth, look at me and make sure you hear and understand every instruction I am giving you at this time." That was my personal warning from my Mother to stop what I was doing, ignore present distractions, and become attentive. Similarly, God is saying to us, as His children, "Hey kids, be quiet, close your mouth, look at Me and make sure you hear and understand every instruction I am giving you at this time." Our eyes and our ears are the gatekeepers to our hearts. The passage goes on to say, "…keep your heart, with all diligence, for out of it spring the issues of life." The word 'keep' can be used interchangeable with the word, *'guard'* or the word *'protect'*. The Lord is urging and persuading us to protect and guard our hearts, because our hearts contain our destiny.

My Pastor, Dr. Michael Freeman says it this way: "Your heart is the birthplace of all your increase." In other words, you are a brand new laptop computer with unlimited memory; however, programs have not yet been downloaded into your memory. You, as an awesome creation of the Most-High God, have been designed with impeccable hardware. You will automatically and efficiently carry out the information and software that is formatted into your system. Your eyes and ears are the primary channel by which new software becomes formatted into your system. Your heart has unlimited memory, as well, and it will produce results based upon the quality of the software and programming that has been inputted via the ear gate and eye gate.

Protecting my ear gate, or being cautious of the things I listen to, has been a journey for me. I am selective about listening to certain categories of music, because of the lyrics within the music. I grew up listening to all kinds of music: R&B, symphonic, jazz, hip-hop, rap, classical, gospel, etc. When I became serious about my relationship with the Lord, I began to question the impact that certain lyrics within these genres of music had on my life, based upon my understanding of this scripture. I was very attached to some secular artists. I loved their music, their stage presence and their talent. However, their lyrics did not glorify God and their lyrics had now become software that I did not want to remain in my system. For example, one of my favorite artists from the past had a song that is still very popular today. The song's lyrics stated, "I don't see nothing wrong, with a little bump and grind." On the contrary, there is *'plenty'* wrong, "with a little bump and grind." To put it bluntly, now that I was saved and trying to live for God, this particular song totally contradicted everything my Pastors, my church and the Word of God was instructing me. This song was basically trying to encourage me to disobey God, disrespect my body and view the activity "bumping and grinding", as an acceptable alternative to sexual intercourse. How ridiculous! I could not hear the Word of God on Sunday and expect to live it out Monday thru Saturday, while listening to music throughout the week that subtly (or not so subtly) taught me to do otherwise.

Music is so powerful! Music can make you happy one minute and sad the next. In a conducive environment, the right music can make you do some things that you never intended to do and will regret doing, later. Music is used in shopping environments to convert non-shopping customers into happy, money-spending customers. God created music and He is fully aware of the power it possesses. For this reason, every genre of music, whether hip-hop, R&B, country, rock, classical, reggae, jazz and the like, was created to glorify Him. My focus with any music I listen to, are the lyrics. Your focus should be on the lyrics, as well, if we keep Proverbs 4:21-23 in mind. I am not a secular music 'hater', but I am very cautious with material that does not glorify God or promote holiness.

Enough said. You decide for yourself. I made this decision at approximately 19-years-old and I have not regretted it. I am not obsessive-compulsive about this. I do not leave a store if I hear certain music, and I do not try to act 'holier than thou' with other people about it. This is a personal decision, led of the Holy Spirit, for me. I share this principle in this book, because I know that it has certainly helped me dodge avoidable temptations, tests and trials, especially in the area of my sexuality. I listen to all kinds of Christian/gospel music. From hip-hop to jazz, I still listen to it, but the message behind the lyrics and the hot beat, glorifies God.

Guarding your eye gate consists of being cautious about the movies, music videos, televisions shows, cable channels, and DVD's, etc... you watch. Again, your eyes are an entry into your heart and your heart is the place where your personal destiny is born. The material that is exposed to your heart will reappear in your life at some point later on. For example, exposure to pornography and certain music videos create an appetite for lust. The original seed that creates a harvest of masturbation, homosexuality, adultery, fornication and depression can begin with the first exposure. What are you 'watching' or 'exposing' yourself to on a consistent basis? Are you feeding your 'spirit' man or are you feeding your 'flesh' man? The strong man will win. Trying to please God is very difficult, if not impossible, when your visual stimuli are contrary to the Word of God. Certain movies, certain plays and certain programming may hinder your progress and growth as a believer. Material that bothers and challenges me may not be the same for you, but that is why God has given us His Holy Spirit.

Psalms 139:23-24 says, "Search me, O God, and know my heart; Try me, and know my anxieties, and see if there is any wicked way in me, and lead me in the way everlasting." God certainly knows our personal weaknesses, but you should become familiar with your own weakness, as well. I personally, can not handle heavy exposure to explicit sexual scenes, because they cause me to get anxious, restless and hormonally out of control, at times. My mind starts roaming...yikes! Then, I have to start casting down thoughts and images about things that are not of God, according to 2 Corinthians 10: 5-6. Why engage in the mental battle? We already have enough mental battles, without adding fuel to the fire. Be honest with yourself about your own personal weaknesses and respond accordingly.

He will lead and guide us in proper decision-making as it pertains to certain 'viewing' that we can not personally handle. Whether it is explicit sex, violence, perversion, witchcraft, pornography or the like, regardless of your age you must make a decision to guard your eye gate, if you desire to fulfill God's awesome plan for your life. I still love to go to the movies, theatre and rent DVDs. I do watch certain television shows and movies that have explicit scenes, but I am also mindful of the gentle unction I may get from Holy Spirit, if something becomes overwhelming for me. I turn it off. I am not a punk! Nor am I a loser. I am a wise investor, who is carefully considering the consequences of 'this risky exposure' and its effect on my future profits. Trust me. Your heart is the birthplace for your dreams, your desires and your destiny. To guard your heart, is the guard your destiny.

HONOR YOUR FATHER AND MOTHER/ SPIRITUAL PARENTS/PASTORS

This is a powerful principle that will certainly keep you out of trouble. Growing up, I was a smart kid with a smart mouth. Overall, I was pretty decent in the obedience department, but when I did not get my own way I would roll my eyes, twist my neck, suck my teeth and find myself getting put on 'punishment', until I had learned my lesson. This behavior matured during my adolescent and early young adult years. Ephesians 6:2, 3 states, "Honor your Father and Mother, for this is a commandment with promise, that it may be well with you, and you will live a long life, upon the earth." We commonly honor our parents/Pastors on their birthdays, anniversaries and holidays, but one of the greatest ways we can honor them is actually our obedience. I found that it was easy to honor my parents with cards, but the obedience factor was a challenge at times; especially during the times when I wanted to do *my thing*.

Curfews and Lindsay did not mix. I would get home just in time to make curfew, but I would hate having to leave what I was doing...or what I should not have been doing. I had become very cunning at telling my Mom that I was going to be at a female friend's house, while making big plans to be at my boyfriend's house. Basically, I had become a good liar, when it was convenient for me. I was placing myself in a very dangerous position. Through my disobedience, I found myself in clubs, cars, houses and predicaments, I wish I had never encountered. I realize now, that there is safety and divine protection in the will of God. Obedience, even to your parents and Pastors, keeps you in the will of God. Conversely, your disobedience may allow an open door for the enemy, as John 10:10 states, "...to steal, kill and destroy." The enemy would love to seize any opportunity to cause chaos in the life of one of God's own. I opened the door to such chaos, by lying to my Mother, stating that I was going to be in one location, only to be in another location with my boyfriend.

Young adults do this constantly, but do not see the consequences behind their decisions. There are countless car accidents, drive-by shootings, misdemeanors, pregnancies, rapes, and other unfortunate experiences that could have been prevented by one simple act of obedience. Our parents, Pastors and mentors act as transitional safeguards, intercessors, and coverings in our lives at various ages and stages. As a young, single adult, I still honor and respect my parents, but it is no longer in the form of a curfew. My Pastors and mentors have the permission to correct me and challenge me now. I honor their position in my life, and respond accordingly. You should identify the parents, Pastors and mentors in your life. Regardless of how you may feel, during the critical moments when they say 'no' or disagree with you, they really have your best interest at heart. Trust me. Obedience is better than sacrifice (1 Samuel 15:22). Obedience today (for all ages), will prevent headache and heartache tomorrow.

HANG WITH PEOPLE WHO HAVE YOUR ANSWER, AND GET AWAY FROM PEOPLE WHO HAVE YOUR PROBLEM

This principle is my Pastor's personal motto. You may have also heard the sayings, "Birds of a feather flock together", "You are known by the company you keep," or "It only takes one rotten apple to spoil the whole bunch." Well, it is so true! The Bible goes on to make this principle explicitly clear. Please refer to these three references.

1) 1Corinthians 15: 33 "Do not be deceived, evil company corrupts good habits."

2) Proverbs 12:26 "The righteous should choose his friends carefully..."

3) Proverbs 13:20 "He who walks with wise men will be wise, but the companion of fools will be destroyed."

Your friends are a major influence in your life. We can become very impressionable around people whom we admire, respect and trust. There are some good influences, as well as bad influences that exist in everyone's life. Your goal is to identify the bad influences or 'people that have your problems' and separate yourself from the negative effect they have on your everyday choices. The scripture in 1Cor.15: 33 cautions us with a simple statement, "Do not be deceived". In other words, do not be tricked, fooled, or taken advantage of, in this matter concerning your friendships and associations. "Evil company" is referring to friendships, mentors and associations that do not encourage your whole-hearted pursuit of the will of God for your life.

For example, as a freshman in undergrad, I had a friend that encouraged me to go to this guy's room one night after leaving a club. I liked him and he liked me...well, he liked my body, anyway. He was casually flirtatious with me and my friend encouraged me to respond. As a naïve freshman, I let this guy take advantage of me and I never really heard a word from him thereafter. I did not have sex with him, but I felt like I did. I was in way over my head with this guy, because he did not know me enough to respect my boundaries, (even if my boundaries at that time were still outside of the will of God.) Fortunately, I was not physically forced to do anything I did not want to do, but mentally, I felt the pressure to perform at a higher sexual level, now that I was in college. I felt a pressure that night, to do more. I wish that a friend or associate who loved God or at least expected more from me, could have accompanied me that evening, I probably would have never set foot in that dorm room. This is why Proverbs 12:26 urges us to select our friends with caution and great care. Maybe some would say that I should have been strong enough to make my own decision against going into the guy's room and furthermore, against having any form of sexual interaction with him. However as you know, sometimes we get caught up in the moment.

Sometimes, we simply go with the flow. Sometimes we simply follow the leader, and do what we see others doing. Sometimes we have a brain freeze and begin to think with our hormones. If any of these things happen to you (which they will at some point), you need an efficient back-up system of good friends and righteous counsel. This particular friend was not a Christian. She was rebellious in her own right and her sense of adventure and fun was far more advanced than mine. She became 'evil company' in my life, and this was difficult for me to recognize at the time, because of the deception of her so-called friendship. It can be difficult to sever relationships, but eventually if you do not properly address them the Bible says, "…the companion of fools will be destroyed," and according to 1 Corinthians, your good habits will be destroyed as well. You may be a good person, headed in the right direction with great purpose, but the wrong friendships and associations have the potential to destroy your life, one rotten apple at a time.

Now, I adhere to the scripture. I choose my friends carefully and associate with wise individuals. You should find other young men and women who have decided to wholeheartedly pursue God's purpose and plan for their lives, including their sex lives. Amos 3:3 states, "Can two walk together unless they are agreed?" How can you decide to live holy, embrace God's word and save yourself for your wife/

husband, while your so-called best friend is clubbing, getting his/her freak on every night and not sparing any of the details? How? Either your friend is going to get saved and change his/her lifestyle, or you are going to get 'turned-out', and known as the Christian hypocrite. Do not kid yourself here! Do not be deceived. Hang with people who have your answer and get away from people who have your problem.

PURSUE SEXUAL PURITY

In chapter 3, Male/Female Interactions, I addressed the topic of sexual purity from the aspect of a brother-sister relationship. You may want to revisit that chapter for a quick refresher course, before digging into another aspect of this principle. I can recall being aware of 'sexual' curiosity and desires as early as the 5th grade. Sexual education was formally taught in our school district at this grade level, but I also remember my own natural curiosities awakening around this time, as well. In my household, I was allowed to have telephone conversations with males at age 13. I was allowed to have male company at age 15. I was allowed to date and ride in a male's car, at age 16. When I started dating, my curfew was midnight. As a high school senior, it was extended to 1:00 am, or what was seen as appropriate. These were my Parents rules. My Mom did her best to shield me from 'boys' until I was 'mature' enough to handle the drama that came along with them. Maybe your parents' rules were/are a little different, nevertheless, their views have influenced your interactions with the opposite sex in some way. I look back and I thank God, even for these parameters.

Through my rearing, my Mom instilled in me the ability to expect more freedom and opportunity, as I matured and could handle the responsibility that went along with it. I learned a lesson on the importance of establishing guidelines, (even though I found clever ways to bypass them). In a sense, this eager anticipation of new male-female privileges helped me remain focused with my academic and athletic endeavors, household chores, personal attitude and behavior. At times, however, it became frustrating to wait for these privileges and opportunities, especially when it seemed like everyone else my age, was already talking on the phone, dating, riding in cars, and having 'male' company. Even now, it can become frustrating at times, to wait for the privileges and benefits of an exciting, eagerly anticipated married sex life. Yet, God has given me this life-changing revelation about waiting: I am worth the wait! My husband is worth the wait. You too, are worth the wait! Allow me to be perfectly honest with you. I want to have sex too! Yes, the minister wants to have sex! I am not stuttering or writing this by accident. I want you to know that God has given us this desire and it is a good desire. In the proper season and His timing, this desire will be fulfilled. Until then, we protect this desire.

In this section on sexual purity I want to address some of the 'sticky' situations that many young adults find themselves in. I am writing this book to liberate you to truly enjoy the life and lifestyle Jesus died for you to have. 1 Thessalonians 5:22 states, "Abstain from every form of evil." Paul addresses the Corinthian church in 1Corinthians 6:12 saying, "All things are lawful for me, but all things are not helpful. All things are lawful for me, but I will not be brought under the power of any." The Living Bible has quite a powerful translation of the same text: "I can do anything I want to if Christ has not said no, but some of these things are not good for me. Even if I am allowed to do them, I'll refuse to if I think they might get such a grip on me that I can't easily stop when I want to." Finally, The Message Bible makes this scripture crystal clear: "Just because something is technically legal doesn't mean that it's spiritually appropriate. If I went around doing whatever I thought I could get by with, I'd be a slave to my whims."

As Christians and children of a wonderful Heavenly Father, God has called us to an intimate relationship with Him through and by His Son, Jesus. Christianity is about a relationship, not a religion. Religion defines a list of do's and don'ts, and puts people in bondage to its manmade rules and regulations. This principle on sexual purity is not about you developing a list of do's and don'ts, but rather about you developing your intimacy with God, through and by His Word and His Spirit. As you learn His Word, you will become more acquainted with His voice. He wants to speak to you, like He would speak to a friend. God has called you to know Him, intimately.

Your true relationship with God will maintain your sexual purity at any age or stage of your life. Let me explain. Romans 8:14 says, "For as many as are led by the Spirit of God, these are the sons of God." I have had instances when I knew that the Holy Spirit was leading me to leave a club, drive my own car on a date, not give my phone number to a guy, or to double-date versus a one-on-one situation. The list goes on. Each of His gentle instructions are His way of leading and guiding me in making proper choices that will glorify Him and keep me from a place of compromise. Like Paul explained to the Corinthian church, I am also explaining to you, I *could* go clubbing, sip wine here and there, entertain sexual appetizers, and enjoy a platonic sleepover or two, because it seems *allowable* under the guise of religion, but I choose to abstain from anything that could remotely appear to dishonor God.

Here is my *personal version* of 1 Corinthians 6:12, as it pertains to your personal walk with God. "You can do anything you want to, if Christ has not said no (officially, by the written letter of the word), but some of these things are not good for you, (because they introduce greater opportunities for weakness to sin). Even if you are allowed to do them (because a specific scriptural reference does not exist to advise you otherwise), you should refuse to if you think they might get such a grip on you that you could not easily stop when you want to (being free of the consequences and influences you have been exposed to)". In other words, let the Holy Spirit lead you, even in what may seem to be the insignificant choices of your personal life. He longs to speak to us concerning the big things, as well as the little things. My point is this: God may be telling you to stop clubbing, stop flirting, stop sneaking, stop masturbating, stop humping, stop participating in oral sex...the list goes on. You must be sensitive enough to the Spirit of God that when He begins to convict your heart about a certain matter, you simply follow and obey. You are not led by a religion; you are led by a relationship.

Now, let me take some time to address those sticky situations I mentioned earlier.

Sticky situation #1) The Sleepover

The sleepover can be defined as any extended period of time 'overnight', with your friend of the opposite sex. It can take place at any residence (apartment, dorm, parent's house, friend's house, hotel, etc)…when all parties involved decide to take a nap, spend the night, or simply stay over until morning, usually with no formal intention of sexual interaction. The sleepover is a major set-up for *badness*! I have had my share of sleepovers and none of them were innocent. I mention 'the sleepover' in this section, because if you have not been presented with this situation, I guarantee that an opportunity will come your way one day. When striving for sexual purity you need to be aware of situations that may give rise to sexual impurity.

The sleepover creates an atmosphere that is conducive to fulfilling your sexual appetite in subtle ways. I can recall one particular sleepover that happened in college. Like most sleepovers, it was not intended. I was hanging out with a group of people, and eventually coupled off with a male friend. As the evening progressed, I was left without transportation to get home. I could have taken a taxi, but instead I chose to hang out for a *sleepover.* (Set-up)! Keep in mind, he was only a friend. Well, I had been attracted to him in the past, and maybe I still was. I did not think he would try anything crazy or inappropriate with me, but maybe (secretly), my flesh (sinful nature) wanted him to. Nothing happened,

49

thank God. Yet, we both knew that the 'opportunity' and the 'attraction' were mutual.

We must be honest with ourselves. Seriously! Our flesh can secretly be seeking sexual fulfillment and then we take it to an all-you-can-eat-buffet, like a sleepover! (Set-up!) Those little hugs, light kisses, affectionate rubs and playful wrestling matches can lead to more than you bargained for. The Living Bible makes it pretty plain, in Roman 13:14. It states, "but let the Lord Jesus Christ take control of you, and don't think of ways to indulge your evil desires." In past times, I have repented of premeditated, highly calculated episodes of 100% lust. Yikes! There is an official list of crazy thoughts you contemplate during a sleepover:

- Where will he sleep?

- Where will I sleep?

- What if he tries to flirt with me?

- Should I try to get close to her?

- Should we stay up and talk all night?

- Is he going to look at me differently because I am sleeping over?

- Should I really be doing this?

- Is there a scripture that says I can not do this?

- Should we stay in the same room? The same bed?

- Because we are just friends, we can handle being in the same bed, right?

- Do I have any condoms, just in case?

- I wonder if I can get her to take her clothes off?

- I wonder if people will think that we have had sex, just because of the sleepover.

The list goes on and on. This is why a sleepover is always a bad idea. It stimulates your mind toward sexual impurity. In one sense, it is a perfect set-up for fornication. God gave us a perfect commandment regarding fornication. Flee! Run! 1Cor. 6:18 says, "Flee sexual immorality." The Living Bible translation says, "…run from sex sin." The sleepover can be dangerous ground.

The sleepover can happen in various ways. It can happen after a late night of group studying, after a date, after an out-of-town visit or party. Beware of the sleepovers that take place with your boyfriend or girlfriend. Run! One of my sleepovers ended in a night of flirtation, only. Another one or two, (or several) have been premeditated, highly calculated episodes of pure lust. One sleepover, in particular went pretty bad, giving opportunity for sexual compromise, which I did not *flee* from, but rather welcomed. I remember regretting this episode especially, because I not only compromised on the standard I had set for myself, but I also disrespected my parents' home. I was in bondage for months, because of one dumb decision (and I was born-again and filled with the Spirit at this time). Thank God for 1 John 1:9 which states, "If we confess our sins, he is faithful and just to forgive us our sins, and to cleanse us from all unrighteousness." God will always give you a second, third, fourth and fifth chance! But honestly, why put yourself in that position? You make dumb decisions during sleepovers. Trust me. Do not even put yourself in this situation, folks. It is a set-up!

Sticky situation #2) club/party

Again, this section is dedicated to revealing some of the sticky situations that can arise from this atmosphere. I am, by no means, trying to put you in a box and tell you how to live your life. Life is choice driven, and you live or die, by the choices you personally make, on a daily basis. My goal here is to inform those who truly have a desire to remain sexually pure. All clubs and parties are not created equal. There are some exceptions to the rule. At this stage in my life, I personally, am not a clubber/party-hopping person. Out of my parents' house, away in school and without a curfew, is when my official party stage began. Washington, DC is a party city, and I became heavily involved in the party scene at that time in my life. The clubs and the parties were the official 'welcome week' events on-campus and throughout the city. However, this season was pretty short lived.

In the beginning, I really enjoyed the club scene. I would make sure that I was really cute, get together with my crew, and we would get to our destination. I love to dance, and I would attract men to come join me or ask me to dance. Now, here is where it gets tricky. Many people do not know how to dance with you without trying to violate you at the same time. Is it dancing, or is it freaking? Is it dancing, or is it four-play? It can be hard to strive for sexual purity while letting someone hump you on the dance floor or while receiving a lap dance. (No pun intended.) This is why a club or party scene can be a sticky situation. Do not misunderstand me.

I love to have fun, but this kind of fun is shaky ground. I love to dance, but this kind of dancing does not glorify God at all. God created all dance, from hip-hop to jazz and ballet, to glorify Him. However, according to Myles Monroe, when the purpose of a thing is unknown, abuse is inevitable. Unfortunately, dancing has fallen prey to this very concept. A club is a prime example of abuse in progress.

One night, I was walking down the hallway in a club, and a guy who I had never seen before in my life, felt comfortable enough to grab my butt as I walked pass him. (Excuse me ladies, my rear end). I thought to myself, he must be insane or mentally challenged, because no one should be sexually violating and degrading women, just for the purpose of generating attention. Additionally, the consumption of alcohol on his part, made a bad situation worse. Excessive alcohol always seems to ignite ignorance. This atmosphere became way too aggressive and intense for my taste. Furthermore, as my relationship with the Lord began to grow, God began to speak to me about multiple areas of my life...including the club/party scene. My taste in music changed, as I mentioned in the section on *"Guarding your Heart"*. My eyes were opened to see that I probably would not be meeting my husband at a club. Nor was I going to meet him on the dance floor, while sweating my hair out, and passing my number to him.

As I stated before, all clubs and parties are not created equal. I attend certain functions, whether they are receptions, galas, dinner parties, birthday parties or graduation parties, but I always allow the peace of God to be the final decision-maker. If I do not really feel comfortable about a certain event,

I may pass on it. If I end up going despite the lack of peace, I usually end up coming home early. You should allow the Holy Spirit to deal with your heart about these matters, as well. I am not trying to be a 'party-pooper' or a 'holy-roller'. I want you to have fun and enjoy life! My motive however, is to challenge you to go to the next level.

BUILD YOUR SELF-ESTEEM AROUND THE WORD

This principle is based upon my observance of others and how they relate their personal value to their possessions, accomplishments and relationships. I encourage you, however, to build your self-esteem, self-worth and self-image around the Word of God. I see many people establishing their self-esteem around their educational accomplishments, athletic abilities, scholarships, awards, degrees, and other accolades. Some young women gain a sense of value when they wear the latest jewelry, clothes, shoes or make-up. Still others have their self-esteem rooted in the presence of a boyfriend or girlfriend in their lives. A fine girlfriend, nice car and hot gear, is all it takes to make some young men feel validated and confident. I personally, could build my self-esteem around many different factors: being a doctor, driving a BMW, my home, my business, my clothes, my book, etc. These are all good things, but these things do not 'make' me. I only have these things through and by God's grace. You have what you have, through and by His grace, as well. I believe that when you begin to truly discover who you are, in Christ Jesus, you begin the journey to the real foundation for your self-esteem.

Your self-esteem and self-image should not be based upon 'things'; it should be based upon your revelation of who you are according to the Word.

1Peter 2:9 states, "But you are a chosen generation, royal priesthood, a holy nation, a peculiar people, that you should show forth the praises of Him Who has called you out of darkness into His marvelous light." The word 'chosen' denotes that God, Himself, has specifically selected *you* above others. He has selected you from among your peers in this generation. The word 'royal' implies that God, Himself, has called you to be a king or queen, and given you an established level of prestige, honor, respect and power. The word 'holy', simply means that you are indeed, set-apart from others to glorify God, and should not try to conform to a lower standard of living. Lastly, the word 'peculiar' signifies God's way of calling you uncommon, unique, unusual, and extremely special.

You are chosen, you are royal, you are holy and you are peculiar. Having a boyfriend does not make you special. Having a boyfriend that spends his money on you does not make you special, either. Having sex and flirting with a bunch of different females does not make you 'the man'. Being 'a player' is not cool, fellas. *True sexiness* is found in being a real man or woman of God! It is time to build our self-esteem around God's word, instead of the information we have learned in the locker room, barbershop, cafeteria, sleepovers and music videos. God established our identity in His Word before the foundation of the world so that we would be complete in Him (Col. 2:10), free from any external means of validation. When you begin to understand the true meaning of the price that

Jesus paid for you on Calvary to make you a virtuous woman or a mighty man of valor, you will stop selling yourself short at a discounted price. Too many Christians are giving out discounts! Make a decision today, to end the discounts. Jesus did not die on the cross to make you a 'Value City'; he died on the cross to make you a 'Neiman Marcus'.

You are truly amazing! Jesus considered you and I, worth dying for.

Psalms 139: 14-16 in the Message Bible states,

"I thank you High God, You're breathtaking! Body and soul, I am marvelously made! I worship in adoration. What a creation! You know me inside out, you know every bone in my body; you know exactly how I was made, bit-by-bit. How I was sculpted from nothing into something. Like an open book you watched me grow from conception to birth; all the stages of my life were spread out before you. The days of my life all prepared before I'd even lived one day."

You are awesome, simply because you are God's handmade creation. There is no one like you. From your fingerprints to your DNA, all of creation would not be the same without you.

You are so special to God, that he allowed two complete strangers (your parents), to come together, to conceive you. Regardless of the circumstances of your birth, or birth family, you are God's miracle, fearfully and wonderfully made. Regardless of what your Mother or Father has said or done, you are not a mistake or a statistic. All depression, insecurities and low self-esteem are covered by the blood of Jesus. Meditate on these scriptures and saturate your thinking with the Word. You may need to read this book several times, until the heart of the message really registers in your spirit. Allow His Word to transform the perception you have of yourself. Build your self-esteem around the Word of God.

DECIDE TO COME TO CHURCH AND BIBLE STUDY (AND OTHER SESSIONS THAT PROMOTE SPIRITUAL GROWTH)

It is absolutely imperative that you place yourself in a good Bible-believing, Bible-teaching environment, with Pastors who truly love people and challenge them to live out the Word of God on a 100-fold level. The 100-fold level is the maximum level at which the Word can be taught, with practical life application, calling for total and complete obedience to godly principles, with understanding. I could fill this book with a 'watered-down' message advocating the use of condoms, masturbation and birth control pills, but none of these methods honor God, nor do they have a scriptural foundation. I love my Pastors, because they challenge me to live life at the 100-fold level. I am challenging you to do the same.

My Pastors 'stretch' me to live my life at the maximum level that God's word requires, and in turn, I can expect the maximum benefit that automatically corresponds with my obedience. My Pastor has an interesting saying: "People *live* at the level they are taught. If people *knew* better, they would *do* better." It is so true. I live the level of lifestyle I am experiencing today, because I am taught the Word of God at the maximum level, on a consistent basis. Additionally, I have disciplined myself to stay within this environment, by consistently attending church, Bible study and other events that foster spiritual principles founded in the Word.

Hosea 4:6 says, "My people are destroyed for a lack of knowledge: because you have rejected knowledge, I will also reject you, that you should not be priest for me: seeing you have forgotten the law of your God, I will also forget your children." What a powerful scripture! God said, "My people", not the heathen, gentile, secular, worldly people. Christians! Churchgoers, tongue-talkers, pew-warmers, Sunday-school-goers and the like are destroyed because of a lack of knowledge. As a Christian, you can go through so much turmoil, simply because you lack some basic information from the Word of God. If you are not being spiritually fed at your church where you can understand the Word and apply it to your everyday life, strongly consider making a change. According to this scripture, your very life depends on it. However, this chapter goes on to describe a group of Christians who are being appropriately fed scriptural principals, but they *reject* the life-application of the principles ministered to them. Is this scripture talking about you? Rejecting God's word is dangerous, because it not only affects you, but it also affects your children. Make a decision to hear God's Word and do it. Stop playing games with God and church! Some people are more committed to their sports team, the nightclub, or their civic, political and social organizations, than they are to their local church and Pastor. Let us keep first things, first.

We come to church, Bible study and various other learning sessions in the Word to transform our way of thinking. We need all of the junk from television shows, radio stations, videos, and locker rooms deprogrammed from our minds. Romans 12: 1, 2 says,

> "I beseech you, therefore brethren by the mercies of God, that you present your bodies to God, a living sacrifice, holy, acceptable to God, which is your reasonable service. And, be not conformed to this world, but be transformed by the renewing of your mind, that you might prove what is that good, acceptable, and perfect will of God."

In pursuing the goal of sexual purity you must continue the 'renewing of your mind' process. It is a process. Trust the process. God is faithful. I did not get 'it' overnight, but I eventually got 'it'. Overtime day-by-day, step by step I began to understand sexual purity, holy living, honoring authority, and the mind renewal process. You will, too. This is why you must make yourself accountable for Word sessions that you miss, due to scheduling conflicts. The Word you miss could be the very Word from God, to revolutionize your thinking and your understanding. Particularly, if your church offers a session for 'singles' only, 'teenagers' only, or 'college students' only, it is to your advantage to attend these meetings, because they will speak to your specific needs and issues. Do not run *from* these sessions, run *to* these sessions. Trust me. You will be happy you did, in the long run.

GET A VISION

I discuss the principle of having a vision in Chapter 5. I focus primarily on discussing my visions and some of the dreams that God has given me. However, I want to focus on you, for now. (Go get a pen, paper and your thinking cap.) Ok. What are your visions? (Start writing now.) 'Where' do you see yourself this time, next year? Five years from now? Ten? What are you *honestly* doing to mobilize yourself toward that place you see in your vision? This may not be your season to entertain a male/female relationship. This may be your season to fully explore your purpose and maximize your single state. The number of young people and young adults that either have no vision for themselves, or completely lack the motivation to achieve 'more' disturbs me. Furthermore, there are those who have certain goals and visions, yet perpetually make decisions that derail their purpose. (They select the wrong job, the wrong boyfriend, the wrong offer, the wrong associates, the wrong church, the wrong attitude, and the wrong advice). Are you involved in a relationship that is distracting you from being 'everything' that God has called you to be?

Get a vision from God and be determined to see it come to pass. There is a lost and dying world that needs to hear your poetry, sing your songs, read your books, utilize your inventions, invest in your business, receive your ministry, admire your artwork, celebrate your architecture, explore your legal expertise, and experience your academic contributions. You are here now, in the earth, by God's perfect purpose and design. You are important and you are necessary! God needs you! The dreams, visions and aspirations that you have will bring you fulfillment, but more importantly, they will supply a greater need for humanity. Those dreams, visions and aspirations help define your purpose. What are you passionate about? What makes you angry? What makes you sad? What inspires you? What do you enjoy so much, that you would do it everyday, even if you did not get paid? The answers to these questions will help you discover your purpose. You must then *choose* to fulfill your purpose. Clearly, the choices I made at 18, 19 and 20 years old (good or bad), have directly impacted the conditions of life I have experienced at 27, 28 and 29 years old. Where you are today, is a summary of the choices you have made in your past. Nothing just happens. You must seek God. The greatest vision you can have in life is to fulfill your God-ordained purpose in the earth.

PRAY CONSISTENTLY

Prayer is a lifestyle. It is a lifestyle of communication with God. You talk to Him, but more importantly, He talks to you. Communication is the key to any relationship. You must develop a lifestyle of acknowledging God, in every area of your life. Jeremiah 33:3 says," Call to Me, and I will answer you, and show you great and mighty things which you do not know." At times, we seek happiness, satisfaction, contentment and fulfillment from our relationships, job, money, education and possessions. The reality of true happiness, satisfaction, contentment and fulfillment is found in a daily decision to seek Him. Even if it starts out as five minutes each day, give God five minutes of private time without distractions. Ladies, the Holy Spirit will reveal to you any knucklehead that you should stay away from, as you develop in a relationship with Him and learn His voice. Guys, the Holy Spirit will show you the sleazy females you should avoid. God will give you strategies to break-away from abusive, unhealthy relationships. God will heal, restore and replenish any area of your life that have been bruised, wounded or scarred by past relationships or abuse. All of these answers are waiting for you in prayer, (in His presence).

I am not using this section to discuss the different kinds of prayer, nor am I using this section to tell you when, how, where and what to pray. You simply need to keep your heart pure and approach God openly. You can come boldly to the throne of grace to obtain mercy and find grace to help you in your time of need, according to Hebrews 4:16. You do *not* need to be a Pastor or a Priest to approach God. God looks forward to you talking to Him in prayer, just as you are. Be yourself. He is not expecting you to sound like your Pastor, mentor, Mother or anyone else. He is looking for you to be real with Him.

Amos 3:3 states, "Can two walk together, except they be agreed?" To walk with God, talk with God and have intimacy with God, you must agree with God. Agreement begins with His Word. You must agree with Him and His Word in prayer. Regardless of what others may say or what statistics may dictate to you, you must establish in your heart that the Word of God is final authority over every area of your life. The Word must be final authority over your single life and your sex life. You must agree that His way is the only way and it is the best way. Condoms, birth control pills, oral sex and masturbation are manmade ways of handling the consequences of sexual promiscuity. I encourage you to invest in a good Word-based prayer book, because it will teach you how to pray the Word of God back to Him and get great results.

CHANGE YOUR ATTITUDE (WALK IN LOVE)

This is a great principle for all of the 'nasty' attitudes we possess, at times. I have experienced too many 'bad' attitudes. I simply got tired of having a bad attitude. Who wants to be mad, upset, tired, depressed, jealous, envious, frustrated and unhappy all the time? Not me! Hopefully, not you, too! I really got tired of being jealous of someone else's clothes, shoes, jewelry, hair, or boyfriend. I got fed up with comparing myself to other people, and feeling like I had to compete with their accomplishments to prove that I was someone important. I got tired of rolling my eyes at other women, acting like I did not see them look my way. It requires too much effort to be 'nasty' toward someone who nine times out of ten, has gone on with their own lives and completely forgotten about why we are mistreating them in the first place. God is challenging us to repent, to apologize to people, to stop holding grudges and to stop wearing our feelings on our sleeve. How can you achieve sexual purity with jealously, frustration, bitterness and anxiety in your heart? Impossible!

What is the solution? The solution is walking in love, according to 1Corinthians13. Examine verses 4 through 8.

"Love suffers long and is patient and kind; love does not envy; love does not parade itself, is not puffed up; does not behave rudely, does not seek its own, is not provoked, thinks no evil; does not rejoice in iniquity, but rejoices in the truth; bears all things, believes all things, hopes all things, endures all things. Love never fails..."

I had to change my attitude and learn to be truly patient and kind with people. After all, God has been patient with me even in the midst of my silliness, ignorance and stupidity.

I learned how to compliment someone else, on their shoes, jewelry, makeup, clothes, promotion, new house or car instead of being jealous of them. You too, must realize that everything God has for you has your name on it. It belongs to you. No one else can take what God has promised you, so just relax! Stop being so anxious! Nobody is going to take your husband, and nobody is going to get your wife, but you. My Pastor says, "If it's God, it won't spoil." Translation: if your relationship with a young man or young woman is a relationship that is born of God, and meant to be, it will be. One year from now, three years from now, or ten years from now...your relationship will not spoil. Be easy! No need for competition or comparison, fellas. And ladies, no need for being 'catty', we are sisters in the Lord. Your destiny, dreams, and desires are tailor-made, just for you. We can be happy for others and put jealously, envy, competition, comparison and judgment aside, when we walk in love.

STOP THE SIN

'It' is an act of your will. You can stop doing 'it' at any time. 'It' truly has no power over you, but the power that you give 'it'. 'It' could be lying, masturbating, sex, shoplifting, cheating on taxes, cursing, unforgiveness, homosexuality, smoking, or any form of disobedience to God. What is really disturbing, is that some people have become so skillful at 'it', they have incorporated 'it' into their everyday lives. You can be absolutely gorgeous and 'it' makes you look ugly. You can be the finest thing since Boris Kodjoe, but 'it' makes you look weak. You can be at the head of your class, at the top of your game, seemingly soaring through life, but 'it' will eventually destroy your life. 1 Corinthians 15:34 says, "Awake to righteousness and do not sin..." I believe that when you get a true eye-opening revelation of the price paid for your righteousness by Jesus Christ, you will begin to hate sin. You will hate the practice of sin, a.k.a. the sin lifestyle. More than that, you will hate the feeling that comes after you have sinned; the conviction, the condemnation and the mental turmoil. You will begin to hate disappointing your Father, who loves you so much.

It is possible to change! You can change, and begin to live the way God originally intended for you to live. One day at a time, and one decision at a time, it is possible for you. As I truly began to grow in love with Jesus at 18 years old, I started the process to eliminate sin from my life, because I honestly wanted to please Him. Religion will definitely allow you to commit the same sin over and over again, while singing in the choir, playing the drums, preaching, leading children's church or ushering. Conversely, *'relationship'* will convict you to leave your girlfriend, change your friends, throw out your condoms and develop in this covenant love with your Heavenly Father. A real relationship with God will keep you out of that 'particular sin' during public settings as well as private encounters. A real relationship with God will cause you to be the same person, privately and publicly. You can stop the sin today!

After you have stopped, check out 1John 1:9. Every believer should know this one. It is the 911 scripture, according to our Youth Pastor, Jeff Wooten. It reads, "If we confess our sins, He is faithful and just to forgive us our sins, and to cleanse us from all unrighteousness." Receive it! It is true! One day at a time and one decision at a time, God has delivered me from my 'dumb' days. I confessed all of the dumb decisions, dumb relationships and dumb disobedience to Him, and He forgave me, as He promised. However, (part two), the cleansing process took some time. It required some mentoring, Bible study time, accountability, submission, prayer, patience and obedience. But, I was worth it, (at least Jesus thought so)! Life is so much better on the other side of sin!

5

The Vision

Vision is a powerful tool. The American Heritage Dictionary defines vision as; 1) the faculty of sight, 2) unusual foresight, 3) a mental image produced by the imagination, 4) seeing the supernatural as if with the eyes, 5) one of extraordinary beauty. I submit to you that a vision is indeed, all these things. It truly is your ability to see. It is your ability to see beyond your present, into your future by the inspiration of the Holy Spirit. It is also unusual foresight that provides a blueprint for your destiny and purpose. It is a mental image that comes alive on the inside of you, as your relationship with God develops and you allow the Holy Spirit to breathe on your imagination. Vision truly allows you to see the supernatural with the eyes of your spirit, despite your present situations and dilemmas. And finally, a vision is definitely something of extraordinary beauty, because it will transform the very nature of your existence. A vision is just that powerful.

Habakkuk 2:2-3 states,"...write the vision, and make it plain on tablets that he may run who reads it. For the vision is yet for an appointed time; but at the end it will speak and not lie. Though it tarries, wait for it; because it will surely come, it will not tarry." God desires for you to have His best in every area, at every age, and every stage of your life. He longs to give us the desires of our heart (Psalms 37:4). He has given us clear instructions to write down our visions, desires and dreams, because at the appointed time, they will manifest in our lives. Writing will provide a means of recording the things you desire from God. Writing should not be a cumbersome task, but rather a joy of detailing the prophetic snapshot you have of your future. God has given us another form of writing the vision, beyond mere pen and paper. Psalms 45:1 states, "my tongue is the pen of a ready writer." My Pastor says it this way, "your mouth is the steering wheel to your destiny." God has put the power of life and death in our mouths, through and by the words that we speak on a daily basis (Proverbs 18:21).

I am a vision-driven, purpose-driven individual. I believe in having a vision for every area of life. I do not have every detail worked out about 'how' it will come to pass, but I release my faith for God's best and trust Him for the results. I had a vision of going to medical school and becoming a doctor ever since I was a young child. In 4th or 5th grade, I went to school as a doctor for 'professional day', because that is what I wanted to be 'when I grew up'. I did an artistic drawing in the 6th grade, displaying the fulfillment of my dream...becoming a doctor. I completed medical school in May 2002 at The George Washington University in Washington, DC. June 2006 marks the completion of my residency in anesthesiology there, as well. God Himself, opened supernatural doors for me to be accepted into medical school at the end of my sophomore year of undergrad at GW. I did not take the MCAT, which is the national exam required for admission to medical school. I share this, because I personally know the power of having a vision, remaining focused and allowing God to do the impossible in your life. In part, this vision enabled me to hold my course throughout the years and maintain my virginity by his grace. Pregnancy, abortion, STD's, distractions and other male-drama could have potentially forfeited my dream. I could not let that happen. That, my friend, is the power of having a vision set before you. What distractions are you allowing to eat away at your destiny?

As I said before, I have a vision for every area of my life. I wrote my vision for a husband, when I was in the 7th or 8th grade. It is amazing to me that even though I did not grow up around the 'Word of Faith', I operated in certain principles of faith without even knowing it. When I came in contact with my Pastors, Drs. Michael and Dee-Dee Freeman, I came in contact with life-changing principles from the Word of God. Furthermore, I began to study on my own. God began to rewrite the vision I prepared for myself, as a child. I developed a vision for the husband God desired for me to have. Someone who compliments my purpose, compliments my appearance, compliments my finances, and compliments the overall plan of God for my life. Proverbs 29:18 states, "Where there is no revelation (vision), the people cast off restraint." In other words, when you lack vision for a particular area of your life, you have no guidelines or established course of action. No road map. No destination. You settle for anything, or anybody that looks good, talks good, drives good and maybe carries a Bible, occasionally. You have no set standard for what you like or dislike. You have no set guidelines for what you will and will not accept in a relationship. Lacking vision can be a dangerous thing.

If you do not have a vision for your future mate, and you desire to be married one day, I suggest you arrange time to write it very soon. It will take some of the stress, strain and struggle out of your male/female relationships. Just to help get you started, I will share a few things I did. I wrote down some of the physical things I desire from God in my future mate. Then I wrote down the spiritual things I desire in a mate.

This is just an example.

PHYSICAL:

- Good-looking, handsome (I love a FINE man.)
- Tall (I like tall)
- Good steward of his body (nice haircut, masculine, good grooming)

- Nice lips (I like lips…ok, what?)
- Nice smile

SPIRITUAL:

- Born-again and filled with the Holy Spirit (without question)
- Pure in heart (Math 5:8)
- Good name (Proverbs 22:1)
- Righteous and walks in integrity (Proverbs 20:7)
- Sharpens me, even as I sharpen him (Proverbs 27:17)
- Wise with his associations (1Cor 15:33)
- Possesses knowledge and quick in understanding (Daniel 1:4)

These are just a few of the items I have listed in my vision, but immediately just these details alone, have begun to paint a picture of a certain individual(s). Although we do not quite know who this individual is, certainly, everybody in the male species does not fit into this category. Certainly, just 'anyone' does not qualify to be my husband, if we simply go by these criteria alone. My criteria exclude those who do not fit the standards set by the vision. How does a Christian young woman 'fall in love' with a young man who is unsaved, unchurched and untaught? How? She lacks vision. No vision. No standards!

This is not a new concept. Universities and programs all over the country use the same principal during the admission selection process. They have certain exclusion criteria they use to separate the few qualified applicants within an applicant pool of thousands. Their criteria consist of a specific SAT/ACT score, essay, recommendations, specific GPA, interview scores, certain extracurricular activities, honors, awards, community service efforts, research opportunities, and the list goes on. The average Ivy League school has very different criteria than your local community or state school. People are not offended by this standard, because there is often a far greater price to pay, to attend one of these institutions, as well. Few high school seniors qualify for admission to an Ivy League school, simply because they do not meet the criteria. Likewise, everybody should not meet the criteria to gain admission into a relationship with you. Once you establish set criteria that come from the Word, you will realize that you probably have a few people in your life, who do not qualify to be there. Jesus died on the cross and became our substitute for sin, so that we would be made the righteousness of God. He died to make you 'Ivy League status.' Yes! There is a greater price tag that comes from being in a relationship with you. An applicant has to work a lot harder and be a lot smarter to gain admission with you, but the education they will gain from being in a relationship with you will be invaluable. Establish your criteria to separate the few qualified perspectives, from the thousands that will continue to apply year after year. Write the vision, today!

There are, however, rare occasions when an Ivy League institution encounters an individual who does not meet all of the criteria for admission, yet they are not immediately rejected from the university. Why? Well, based upon the review of the current application and the information provided, although it lacks fulfillment of all criteria, the potential for this applicant to excel and flourish in a rigorous academic environment is perceived. The admission committee makes a risky decision based upon the *potential* they see in the candidate, despite his/her shortcomings. There may be a rare occasion when this happens to you, as well. You may discern the God-ordained potential hidden within a person, despite what your vision dictates. To grant this person admission into a relationship with you will be a bit of a risk, but if the benefits outweigh the risks, you may have stumbled upon a diamond in the rough. If so, there may be some work ahead, but congratulations on perfecting and polishing your new diamond!

God has a great, tailor-made purpose for your life. It includes your dreams, desires and ambitions, but it also includes the gifts and the talents He has placed on the inside of you to be a blessing to so many others. Your life is much 'bigger' than having a boyfriend. Your life is much bigger than getting married, one day. Your life is much bigger than having sex. Jeremiah 29:11 encourages, "...for I know the thoughts I think toward you, says the Lord, thoughts of peace and not evil, to give you a future and a hope." God has a future for you. He has a future full of greatness and fulfillment. As a result of seeking God first, obeying the Word, holding fast to my vision, God has done supernatural things in my life, in such a short amount of time. Plus, I am single! To God be all the glory! What He has done for me, He will do for you.

From the Mercedes to the BMW, the house, the academics, ministry and the business, this level of life is possible for you, right now!

I am writing this book to let you know that you can remain sexually pure until you are married! Not only that, but you can be happy and fulfilled while doing it. You can be happy during your teenage, college and adult single years. Happiness does not come from homecomings, step shows, clubs, parties and other events. Happiness does not come from things that are 'happening'. Happiness comes from trusting in the Lord and doing the will of God. (Proverbs 16:20, 29:18) Change your perspective. Take the limits off of God and take the limits off of yourself. I believe that now is the time when God wants to do exceedingly, abundantly, above all we can ask or think (Ephesians 3:20). Beyond your education, neighborhood, resources, income, parents, race, gender, stereotypes and age. So I urge you, outline a vision for that special mate, your new house, your finances, career goals, scholarship, ministry, new invention, new book or business. All of the answers are found in the Word of God. It is the foundation for every vision.

6

The Best Sex of My Life

The best sex of my life will happen when I stand before God and my husband on the day of our covenant wedding. I look forward to presenting myself before him as a gift. Not a cheap, discounted, broken gift. Rather, a precious, restored, and priceless gift. I look forward to presenting myself to God, as His daughter, full of purity and integrity, by His grace. In that moment my husband will truly know that, I was worth the wait. I will also fully understand that he was worth the wait. I have carefully thought about what special gift I could offer him on our wedding day. However, my sexual purity will be a special gift to him and him alone. A customized gift, designed, reserved and perfected for Him, only. This gift has come very close to being unwrapped, yet it has endured for one special recipient. How intimate it will be, for us to engage in the great gift exchange: the best sex of my life. I will have my last, 'first kiss'. My Pastor will pronounce, "…and *now*, you may kiss the bride", implying that prior to *now*, kissing was a restricted activity. Properly so, because kissing is intimate and people establish covenants with their mouths. Such a precious thing as kissing should not be taken lightly. It will truly be a monumental time in my life. I have made the decision to reserve and preserve all sexual acts: intercourse, rubbing, touching, kissing and the sexual appetizers, for my husband and our wedding day. God deserves my obedience. He deserves my best. My decision is all about Him and following His perfect order so that He can receive the maximum glory from my life. God is able to keep me. God is able to keep my future mate, wherever he is. God is able to keep you, too!

God created sex! He knows everything about it. He knows how good it is. He knows how much fun it can be. God did not just make us simple creatures of reproduction, but He designed an event called 'sex' with you and I in mind. In the proper context, which is marriage, He wants you to let loose, be free and have an awesome sexual experience with your spouse. God purposed for sex to be a special gift for a man and a woman that have committed their lives to one another. Sex is God's idea!

Trust God. Imagine, even now, he is grooming your wife or husband for the covenant of marriage. He is perfecting their lifestyle, perfecting their language, maturing their thought life, maturing their emotions and increasing their financial status. He is cultivating their heart, building their character, enhancing their worship and sharpening their knowledge of Him. He is polishing their appearance, polishing their style and polishing their charm. DO NOT LIMIT GOD! Believe Him for the best. In the meantime, you should personally aim to be 'the best', as you believe for 'the best'. Our loving Father, the creator of all things, including the sexual experience, will truly be honored, just like He was on the day that He presented the lovely woman to Adam for the very first time. "For this reason a man will leave his father and mother and be united to his wife, and they will become one flesh." (Gen. 2:24 NIV)

THE BEST SEX OF MY LIFE (MY SILLY SIDE)

All jokes aside, I am going to be REALLY READY for my wedding day! I have years of stored up 'expressive energy' that the Lord will finally allow to be free. Thank you, Jesus! Oh, happy day! (And I am *not* talking about when Jesus washed my sins away.) Many women cry during weddings. Why? First of all, I refuse to mess up my $200.00 makeup job. I will have spent too much money on my wedding gown, to get makeup and tear stains on it! Furthermore, I am going to be too happy and hormonal, to cry. I have considered telling my Pastor to do the abridged, cliff notes version of the vows, skip communion and then skip the reception altogether. Who needs the reception? What genius invented the concept called 'the reception', anyway? Skip the eating. Get to the *lov-*

ing! Skip the photos. Get to the *loving*! Skip the gifts. Well, second thought. Receive the gifts quickly, and then get to the *loving*! The reception *should* be held one week after the couple has been married, to ensure that no one interferes with the *'loving'*!

Imagine this! If the reception were a week after the wedding, we would smile really big and be especially friendly to everybody. No one would be mad at the photographer for taking too long with the pictures, and no one would be mad at the wedding coordinator for making us stay late to greet people we barely know. Why? Well, all of the 'expressive energy' would be free at last. If I may borrow the wise words of Dr. Martin Luther King Jr., "free at last, free at last, thank God Almighty the *energy* is free at last." I heard one couple's testimony. They remained sexually pure and waited until their wedding night. All I can describe, is that *'he rocked her world'* in one night. Her family and Pastor recall, she returned home from her honeymoon, *a new creature in Christ*, (and she was already saved, if you know what I mean). Wow! Some would disagree with me, thinking, if I have waited my entire life for 'the best sex of my life', a few more hours of waiting is no big deal. I disagree! *I want my world rocked, too! In Jesus name!*

7

Restoration

The good news of the gospel of Jesus Christ is that, God is a God of restoration, renewal, reconciliation and a second chance. As stated in Joel 2:25, "So I will restore the years that the swarming locust has eaten, the consuming locust and the chewing locust." The blood of the lamb can wash away years of hurt, shame, bitterness and unwise decisions. Times of low self-esteem, low self-worth, and promiscuity can be forgiven by the God who promises to cast our sins as far as the east is from the west (Psalms103: 12). No matter what you have done, whom you have done it with, or why, God loves you and sent His only Son to die for you and I. You are not a failure or an embarrassment. You are a child of the Most High God. God can heal and replenish you even if your sexual purity was violated through rape or molestation. Even in such tragedy and devastation, God promises to give you a renewal and a rebirth of your sexual purity and confidence. You are still royalty. This chapter is an opportunity to rededicate and recommit your life and lifestyle, to the Lord Jesus Christ. If you do not have a relationship with God, through and by His Son, Jesus Christ, there is a brief, yet powerful prayer for salvation, located at the conclusion of this chapter. However, if you are already a born-again believer reading this book, God maybe calling you to a more intimate relationship with Him.

Beyond mere church attendance, and the hustle and bustle of Bible studies, lies a deeper place with God. There is a special place where God longs to reign. That special place is the throne of your heart and soul (mind, will and emotions). As you spend time in God's presence, in His word and with other believers, allow the blood of Jesus to purge your conscience of every dead work of your past, so that you can truly receive this restoration that can only be found in Him (Heb. 9:14). You will not forget those times when you messed up or were violated, but you will experience freedom, acceptance and appreciation of the victory God has given you over the area of your sexuality. We have all blown it, missed the mark, or been hurt at some point in our lives. Ok. So what! Do not allow your past to be the prison that keeps you from entering into the wonderful future that God has for you. "For I know the thoughts I think toward you, says the Lord, thoughts of peace and not evil, to give you an expected end. "(Jeremiah

29:11) God has not given up on you. His thoughts consist of all of the wonderful things He has done for you, even before time began, to bring you to your final destination of greatness.

After the restoration and healing process, you are made whole. You must receive the healing and restoration, by faith. You will not always, 'feel' restored, and you will not always 'feel' healed. Despite your feelings, you must *choose* to receive your wholeness. Despite whom you may run into from your past, stay focused and trust Him. Psalms 37:3,4 states, "Trust in the Lord and do good. Dwell in the land and feed on His faithfulness. Delight yourself also in the Lord and He shall give you the desires of your heart." After this restoration has taken place in your heart and soul, trust God to manifest the desires of your heart. Follow the guide to purity. Live out the '10 choices.'

Remember:

1) Guard your heart

2) Honor your Mother and Father/Pastors/mentors

3) Hang with people who have your answer, and get away from people who have your problem

4) Pursue sexual purity

5) Build your self-esteem around the Word of God

6) Decide to come to church, Bible study and sessions that promote spiritual growth

7) Get a vision: mate, school, profession, future and ministry

8) Pray consistently

9) Change your attitude (walk in love)

10) Stop *the* sin

You are on the road to the best sex of your life, because this journey begins with a pursuit of purity and obedience, one decision at a time. Be ready to experience your last 'first kiss' and the best sex of your life, in God's perfect time.

Prayer for Salvation

Dear God in heaven, I come to you in the name of Jesus. Your word says, "Whoever shall call on the name of the Lord shall be saved" *(Acts 2:21)* Lord, I call on you. I pray and ask Jesus to come into my heart and be Lord over my life according to *Romans 10:9-10.* "If you shall confess with your mouth the Lord Jesus and believe in your heart that God has raised Him from the dead, you shall be saved." Lord, I do this right now. I confess that Jesus is Lord and I believe in my heart that You, God, raised Him from the dead. I am saved. You are now, my Heavenly Father and I am a child of the Most-High God. In Jesus name. Amen.

The Best Sex of My Life: a Guide to Purity

SEXUAL PURITY CONFESSION COVENANT

I, _____, agree to pursue sexual purity as an act of my will. Sexually purity is my personal choice. Therefore, daily, I will make choices that help cultivate and establish the perfect will of God for my life, because I deserve God's best!

I will adhere to the principles I have learned from the Word of God.

1) I choose to guard my heart. I will be mindful of the things I allow myself to be exposed to; from music to movies to videos, I will be selective about what I allow to influence my thinking and decision-making. (Proverbs 4:21-23)

2) I choose to honor my parents, Pastors and mentors, by submitting to godly authority and godly advice. I understand that these people are a part of God's 'protection plan' for my life. (Ephesians 6:2, 3)

3) I choose to hang with people who have my answer, and get away from people who have my problem. (Pastor Mike's Motto) I understand that the companion of fools will be destroyed, so I chose my friends and associates carefully. (1Corinthians 15:33, Proverbs 12:26, and 13:20)

4) I choose to pursue a life of sexual purity. My body is the temple of God. I respect, honor and esteem this temple. I will not defile or abuse it in any way. Therefore, I avoid and turn away from all sexual sin: premarital sex, homosexuality, masturbation, oral sex, 'humping' and/or anything similar! (1Thessalonians 5:22, Romans 8:14, 1Corinthians 6:12)

5) I choose to build my self-esteem around the Word. I am complete in Christ Jesus. My money, my cars, my real estate, my accomplishments, my athletic ability, my positions, my titles, my clothes, my jewelry, and my girlfriend/boyfriend do not 'make' me! The Word of God has established my self-esteem. I am a chosen generation, a royal priesthood and a holy nation. I am fearfully and wonderfully made. I like me! (1Peter 2:9, Colossians 2:9, Psalms 139:14-16)

6) I choose to come to church, bible study and other sessions that promote spiritual growth, because I must stay on the cutting edge of learning and development with my relationship with God. I keep my mind renewed so that I can fulfill the perfect will of God for my life. (Hosea 4:6, Romans 12:1, 2)

7) I choose to be a person with vision. I release my faith for God's best in my future mate, my professional goals, my destiny and my dreams. I choose to remain focused so I will not make decisions I will regret later in life. (Habakkuk 2:2-4, Proverbs 29:18)

8) I choose to pray consistently. I have a relationship with God. I talk to Him about the big things, as well as, the little things. In everything, I acknowledge Him, including male/female relationships. He answers me and makes my path straight and clear. (Jeremiah 33:3)

9) I choose to change my attitude, and walk in the love of God. I have divorced myself from comparison and competition. I have divorced myself from a rebellious attitude. I have divorced myself from being arrogant, prideful and obnoxious. Now that I am mature, I have put away immature things. (1 Corinthians 13)

10) I choose to stop the sin in my life. As an act of my will, I repent and turn away from any activity that does not honor God and my body. I am stronger, I am greater, and I am bigger, than any temptation, test or trial that comes my way, because the Greater One lives on the inside of me. (1 Corinthians 15:34)

I am fully restored and renewed by the blood of Jesus, regardless of my past errors or mistakes. I have a fresh start, in Christ Jesus!

I choose to keep myself sexually pure until the day that I marry God's best for my life! Therefore, I fully expect and anticipate for God, my Father, to give me the desires of my heart because I have followed His instruction. On my wedding day, I fully expect and anticipate THE BEST SEX OF MY LIFE!

In the name of Jesus, my lifestyle is an excellent example for others to follow!!

_____

Signature and date

_____

Witness Signature and date

About the Author

D r. Lindsay Marsh is a young, inspiring woman with a heart to see people: teenagers, college students and singles, experience God's best, and fulfill their destinies, while keeping their own unique 'flavor'. Originally from Shaker Heights, Ohio, Minister Lindsay attended The George Washington University in Washington, D.C. for undergraduate, medical school, and post-graduate training, specializing in anesthesiology.

June 2006 marks the official completion of her residency training in anesthesiology, concluding a long road of intensive training and sacrifice, accomplished only by His grace. She was chosen as an Early Selection Honoree for the School of Medicine, and therefore exempt from taking the national qualifying exam, the MCAT. Yielding to the call of God on her life, she was ordained at the age of 21, became a physician at the age of 25, and began building her first dream home at the age of 27. She openly shares her present triumphs and past struggles of keeping her virginity and living a pure life before God, to provide an example for other believers to follow.

Upon moving to Washington, DC at the age of 18, she connected with her awesome Pastors and mentors Drs. Mike and Dee-Dee Freeman of Spirit of Faith Christian Center, in Temple Hills, MD. At Spirit of Faith, Minister Lindsay serves as one of her Pastors' personal assistants and is director of "Word Up!" a Christian campus outreach designed to focus on college issues like sex, Greek life, relationships, and money management. Minister Lindsay and one of her close friends founded "Word Up!" during their sophomore year of college, providing a bible-believing, bible-teaching resource for their peers. GW awarded her with the 'Excellence in Student Life Award', a campus honor and scholarship acknowledging outstanding student leadership and service within the campus community.

She is also CEO and creative director of *Worth The Wait, LLC* an exciting, new clothing label, which challenges the current standard of our day, by emphasizing and celebrating abstinence. *Worth The Wait* is sexual purity urban expression gear for both men and women. This clothing line is for those who accept the task of representing sexual purity with contemporary style and urban class. Please visit: *www.iamworth-thewait.com* for more information.

She is a leader for S.W.A.T. (Sold-Out Word Activated Teenagers), a radical ministry focused on providing teenagers with real life answers from the Word, to everyday situations, ranging from homosexuality to obedience to parents. She is greatly humbled and appreciative of God's blessing and favor on her life and accepts the challenge of being a 'supermodel' for the kingdom of God. She gives God all the glory and credits her success to Him, her Parents and her Pastors.

JUN 15 2011

9 781412 091572